Categorial Grammars

In the last few years categorial grammars have been the focus of dramatically expanding interest and activity, both theoretical and computational. This book, the first introduction to categorial grammars, is written as an objective critical assessment. Categorial grammars offer a radical alternative to the phrase-structure paradigm, with deep roots in the philosophy of language, logic and algebra. Mary McGee Wood outlines their historical evolution and discusses their formal basis, starting with a quasi-canonical core and considering a number of possible extensions. She also explores their treatment of a number of linguistic phenomena, including passives, raising, discontinuous dependencies and non-constituent co-ordination, as well as such general issues as word order, logic, psychological plausibility and parsing.

This introduction to categorial grammars will be of interest to final year undergraduate and postgraduate students and researchers in current theories of grammar, including comparative, descriptive, and computational linguistics.

Mary McGee Wood is a lecturer in Computer Science at the University of Manchester. She jointly edited *Linguistic Theory and Computer Applications*; her work has appeared in *Recent Developments and Applications of Natural Language Processing* (edited by Jeremy Peckham), and *Categories, Polymorphism and Unification* (edited by Ewan Klein and Johan van Benthem).

Linguistic Theory Guides
General editor Dick Hudson

Relational Grammar
Barry Blake

Current Morphology
Andrew Carstairs-McCarthy

Functional Grammar
Anna Siewierska

Categorial Grammars

Mary McGee Wood

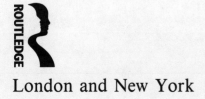

London and New York

First published in 1993
by Routledge
11 New Fetter Lane, London EC4P 4EE

Simultaneously published in the USA and Canada
by Routledge
29 West 35th Street, New York, NY 10001

© 1993 Mary McGee Wood

Typeset in 10/12 pt Times Compugraphic by
MCS Ltd, Salisbury, Wiltshire

Printed in England by TJ Press, Padstow, Cornwall

British Library Cataloguing in Publication Data
Wood, Mary McGee
  Categorial Grammars. − (Linguistic
  Theory Guides Series)
  I. Title II. Series
  415

Library of Congress Cataloging in Publication Data
Wood, Mary McGee.
    Categorial grammars / Mary McGee Wood.
      p. cm. − (Linguistic theory guides)
    Includes bibliographical references and index.
    1. Categorial grammar.   I. Title.   II. Series.
  P161.W66 1993
  415 − dc20   92-21083
                                                        CIP

ISBN 0 415 04954 7
     0 415 04955 5 pbk

for
D m & c

Contents

viii *Contents*

Series editor's preface

The Linguistic Theory Guides have been commissioned with a rather special readership in mind – the typical linguist, who knows a good deal about a small number of theories in his or her area of specialism, but is baffled by the problem of keeping up with other theories even in that area, to say nothing of other areas. There just aren't enough hours in the day to read more widely, and even if there were it wouldn't help much because so much of the literature is simply incomprehensible except to the initiated. The result is that most of us cultivate our own garden reasonably conscientiously, but have very little idea of what is happening in other people's gardens.

This theoretical narrowing is a practical problem if you are expected to teach on a broad front – say, to give a course of lectures on syntactic theory – when you only know one theory of syntax. Honesty demands that one should tell students about alternative approaches, but how can you when you have at best a hazy idea of what most theories have to say? Another practical problem is the danger of missing pearls of wisdom which might be vitally important in one's research, because they happen to have been formulated in terms of some unfamiliar theory. There can be very few linguists who have not rediscovered some wheel in their area of specialism, out of ignorance about work in other theories.

However, there is an even more serious problem at the research level, because one of the main goals of our joint research effort is to work towards the best possible theory (or set of theories), and this can only be done if we constantly compare and evaluate all the available theories. From this perspective, it is simply pointless to spend one's life developing one theory, or some part of it, if it is already outclassed by some other theory. It is true that evaluation of theories is quite a subjective matter, and is far too complex for any kind of absolute certainty to be arrived at. All we can do is to make a reasonably dispassionate, though subjective, assessment of the strengths and weaknesses of the alternatives, in the full expectation that our colleagues may disagree radically with our verdict. Total ignorance of the alternative theories is clearly not a good basis for evaluating them – though it is arguably better than the misinformation that can be used to bolster one's confidence in one's favourite theory.

It is with these problems in mind, then, that we have planned the Linguistic Theory Guides. Each book in the series will focus on one theory that is currently prominent in the literature (or in a few special cases, on a range of such theories). The list of titles is open-ended, and new titles will be added as new theories come into prominence. The aim will be both to inform and to evaluate – to provide enough information to enable the reader to appreciate whatever literature presupposes the theory concerned, and to highlight its strengths and weaknesses. The intention is emphatically not to sell the theory, though the valuation will naturally be sufficiently positive to explain why the theory is worth considering seriously. Several of the theories are already well provided with textbooks which say a great deal about their strengths and very little about their weaknesses. We assume that our typical reader finds such books irritating at best. What they want is clear exposition at the right level of sophistication (i.e. well above first-year undergraduate level), and wise evaluation, both internally and in relation to other theories.

It is not easy to write a book with these qualities, and we have selected our authors with great care. What we have looked for in each case is essentially someone who is a sympathetic outsider, rather than a devotee of the theory – someone who has experience of working within other theories, but who is well-disposed to the theory concerned, and reasonably well-informed about it. We hope that this recipe will produce books which will be acceptably non-partisan in tone, but we have also taken steps to make them factually reliable as descriptions of the theories concerned. Each book has benefited from detailed comment by at least one prominent devotee (a term which we do not apply disparagingly – without their devotees theories would not come into being, still less develop, and there would be no theoretical linguistics), as well as by an outside reader. Needless to say, the authors have been allowed to stick to their evaluations if the protests of their devotee readers have failed to change their minds.

It is our sincere hope that these books will make a significant contribution to the growth and development of our subject, as well as being helpful to those who read them.

Dick Hudson

Acknowledgements

I am more than conventionally grateful to many people for helping to make this book both possible and actual:

Dick Hudson, as series editor, and Dick Oehrle, as technical referee, for meticulous, insightful, constructive comments which have improved the manuscript greatly, and would have even more had I followed them more thoroughly;

Ewan Klein, Mark Steedman, Nigel Vincent and Henk Zeevat, for help with specific points;

Guy Barry, Johan van Benthem, Gosse Bouma, Jack Hoeksema, Michael Moortgat, Glyn Morrill, Dick Oehrle, Remo Pareschi, Mark Steedman, Anna Szabolcsi, Hans Uszkoreit, Kent Wittenburg and others, for sending me many manuscripts and off-prints (not all of which have I been able to incorporate here, much to my regret);

conference audiences, especially in the Linguistics Association of Great Britain, and both colleagues and students at UMIST and Manchester University, notably Guy Barry, Rod Johnson, John Payne, C. J. Rupp, Danny Solomon and Pete Whitelock, for practice in explaining how categorial grammar works and why, and for reassurance that it can be as exciting to others as it is to me;

Claire L'Enfant, Sarah-Jane Woolley and Jenny Potts, for editorial support;

Alan Rector and David Brée, for shelter from the worst potential demands of teaching and administration to give me time for writing;

Penelope Jane and John Chambers, for keeping me sane;

and David, Michael and Christopher, for everything that really matters most, in the end.

1 Introduction

Categorial grammars (CGs) come of a tradition of linguistic description rooted in philosophy of language, logic and algebra, a tradition completely separate, at least for its first forty years or more, from the more prominent constituent-structure tradition. They derive in spirit from the philosophy of Frege (1879, 1891, 1892), explicitly from the logic of Ajdukiewicz (1935), through the algebraic calculus of Lambek (1958). Their view of the underlying nature of natural language is akin to that of dependency grammars, based on the constructive patterns of semantic linkage that hold a sentence together, rather than on the analytic patterns by which it can be segmented.

Categorial grammars are distinctive, though, for their direct representation of semantics in syntax – which endears them to philosophers of language, and to some linguists – and for their arithmetical transparency – which endears them to logicians, and especially to formal and computational linguists. It is no coincidence that the first, abortive flowering of a categorial grammar for serious natural language description came with the first attempts at implementing natural language processing on a computer (Bar-Hillel 1953), and that the true dawn has come with the dramatic rise of computational linguistics, in quantity, quality and contribution to theoretical research, during the last ten years or less.

So, from the point of view of the rest of linguistics, it is high time this book was written. Categorial grammars have insights and methods to offer which are both distinctive and timely, but which, for the most part, lie half-buried from general view in the shifting sands of conference proceedings and university technical reports and dissertations.

From within the categorial enterprise, unfortunately, its timeliness is less obvious. A common core of shared fundamental principles can be identified (and will be discussed in section 1.i). But the realization of those principles, the actual work being done using categorial grammars, is wildly diverse. The main point of consensus in the field at the moment is that the time has not yet come for consensus – as the editors of one of the few readily available sources agree: 'There are many ad hoc proposals flying around, not all of them mutually consistent' (van Benthem 1988b: 29); 'What is called categorial grammar is a rapidly developing field of research for which the time of summarizing its role and achievements seems not to have come yet' (Marciszewski 1988: 7).

This diversity is found on two levels. One should hold for any healthy linguistic theory: for most of the interesting problems in natural language description there are a number of competing explanations in circulation, and the jury is still out (see, for example, the discussions below of gapping (Ch.5.iii.e) and co-ordination (Ch.5.iii.d)). More seriously, the different contributory strands in the categorial tradition remain, to some extent, perceptibly different. There are still some researchers who are clearly really doing algebra, some formal semantics, some natural language syntax; although the mutual respect and influence among them is, on the whole, far greater than it was thirty years ago.

The difference shows even in the embarrassing wealth of different notations in current use (discussed below, Ch.1.iii). This means that a categorial linguist who wants to know just a bit more about the formal properties of a particular categorial grammar, or a formalist who wants some small insight into natural language applications, must each first struggle to learn the notation used by the other for, at heart, the same system. (As this book is intended for linguists, I have used the notation most convenient and common for natural language description, and given references from which the others can be most easily learned.)

Despite this, it is possible and valuable to offer linguists a reasonably clear picture of the principles and current practice of categorial grammars. In the rest of this chapter I shall outline first the most important principles and then the minimal common core of practice of the categorial enterprise. Chapter 2 offers a brief historical introduction, important in understanding what follows. Chapter 3 sets out in detail one widely accepted, 'benchmark' specific categorial grammar, the 'Lambek calculus' (Lambek 1958), and Chapter 4 discusses a range of different proposed extensions to that grammar. Chapter 5 looks at specific proposals for the treatment of a number of significant natural language phenomena, mainly in morphology and syntax, such as derivational morphology, passives and discontinuous dependencies. Chapter 6 covers debates over issues of underlying principle, such as word order and psychological plausibility, and areas of perhaps peripheral interest to the theoretical linguist, such as logic, algebra and computational parsing. Finally, Chapter 7 attempts a summary overview and a forward look at the prospects for categorial grammars, both in their own, internal terms of reference and as an increasingly respected player in the wider game.

I have, at times reluctantly, restricted my coverage here to (relatively) readily accessible material, of primarily linguistic (rather than algebraic or computational) concern. I apologize to all those categorial researchers whose work I have not included; and hope that full-scale publication will become easier and more common for CGs as their momentum continues to grow.

1.i UNDERLYING PRINCIPLES

I began by indicating very briefly two or three of the fundamental principles which importantly distinguish categorial grammars from other linguistic research paradigms: it is time to discuss these more fully.

Categorial grammars offer (in Bar-Hillel's (1953) phrase) a 'quasi-arithmetical notation for syntactic description', or (see Johnson 1987) 'computable linguistic description', combining explicit and precise algebraic characteristics with a close correspondence to the observed semantic and syntactic patterns of natural languages.

Emmon Bach (1987) identifies, across the current diversity of categorial grammars, three defining and unifying principles. First, language is seen in terms of functions and arguments rather than of constituent structure. It is thus a valency or dependency grammar rather than a phrase-structure grammar (PSG); in the literature PSGs and CGs are repeatedly contrasted as (respectively) positional, or configurational, and functional grammars (more on this below).

Second, a very close parallel has traditionally been maintained between syntax and semantics: at least a homomorphism, and in some versions an identity. Commonly referred to as the 'rule-to-rule hypothesis', it can be stronger than that. The claim is not merely that to every rule of syntax there bi-uniquely corresponds a rule of semantics, but that every rule of syntax is, inherently, a rule of semantics. Syntactic description of any complex linguistic unit thus provides for it an integral compositional semantics. The centrality of this principle is generally recognized: Bach (1988: 31) states that 'Probably the one most characteristic and essential feature of both

Montague grammar and categorial grammar is the tight constraint on the relation between syntax and semantics. *A priori* this must count as a point in its favour in comparison with many other theories', and Mark Steedman (1988: 417) that 'The attraction of categorial grammar as a notation for natural language grammar has always been the direct relation that it embodies between the syntax of a language and an applicative semantics.' The homomorphism is discussed most engagingly by Lambek (1988: 312), who in describing the functor Φ: SYNTAX → SEMANTICS refers to a suggestion that 'Φ may be used for catching lions: write the lion's name on a piece of paper and then apply Φ, having first made sure that the paper is inside a cage'.

Taking the somewhat wider family, not all work that one would wish to count as 'categorial' adopts quite as strict a position as the rule-to-rule hypothesis, but it all takes the relation of syntax to semantics (and, indeed, similar relations involving other dimensions, such as phonology) as an issue of critical importance. The school of 'type-driven' linguistic description, for example (e.g. Rooth and Partee 1982; Partee and Rooth 1983; Klein and Sag 1985), and other semantically motivated work, takes a looser, but no less responsible view of the matter. 'Those who are attracted to the project of trying to construct an account of grammatical structure which does justice simultaneously to both grammatical form and grammatical interpretation need not agree in advance on how these (or other) grammatical dimensions interact' (Oehrle, p.c.). They do agree, however, that the question is a central, informing one.

Third, categorial grammars favour monotonicity, avoiding destructive devices such as movement or deletion rules which characterize transformational grammars.

Another important property has been called by Oehrle (1981) 'lexical maximalism' and by Lauri Karttunen (1989) 'radical lexicalism'. Categorial grammars take to its logical extreme the move towards lexical syntax. The syntactic behaviour of any item is directly encoded in its lexical category specification; categories, atomic or complex, replace phrase-structure rules and thus make a separate grammar rule component unnecessary. Bar-Hillel (1953: 61) points out immediately that 'the main economy produced by this method lies ... in that it enables us to dispense completely, at least in principle, with special syntactic statements'. Chomsky (1963: 414) comments that there is a Saussurian position 'that identifies grammar with the set of grammatical properties of words or morphemes (cf. de Saussure 1973: 185–8), and it might reasonably be maintained that [categorial grammar] gives one precise expression to this notion.' In Karttunen's (1989: 44) words, 'A characteristic feature of CG is that the lexical entries of words encode virtually all the information about how words are combined into phrases; there is no separate component of syntactic rules, as is found in most other grammatical frameworks.' In this, of course, categorial grammars represent the extreme form of one of the most widely espoused principles of contemporary linguistics.

They can also be seen as the extreme instantiation of the fundamental Saussurian structuralist principle that 'In language there are no positive terms, only oppositions.' Most linguistic entities are defined, in a categorial grammar, in terms of what they combine with to form what. Rather than 'determiners' there are functions-from-common-nouns-to-NPs, rather than 'transitive verbs' there are functions-from-two-NPs-to-sentences, and so on. The number of basic categories, of things which are defined in terms of themselves, is minimal (even if there are differences of opinion as to what constitutes a minimum). In this way the domain of arbitrary stipulation in a categorial grammar is significantly restricted.

Finally, the richer generalized categorial systems discussed in Chapter 4 offer a flexibility in the structural characterization of complex linguistic objects which makes possible elegant descriptions of those constructions which do not respect canonical 'constituent structure', such as unbounded and discontinuous dependencies (see Ch.5.iii.c) and various co-ordinate constructions (see Ch.5.iii.d). At the extreme of 'structural completeness', for any syntactically coherent string, any substring can be derived as a constituent and any item in that substring as its head. (The linguistic significance of this property is discussed below, Ch.3.v.)

It is worth commenting here on the relation between CGs and PSGs, which has been a significant issue since the two came into use. There is a famous early proof by Bar-Hillel *et al.* (1960) of the weak equivalence of a 'pure' CG to a context-free PSG, which has led to the frequent dismissal of CGs as 'mere notational variants' of PSGs. The *non*-triviality of notational variance is of course a very general point, not restricted to CG or indeed to formal linguistics, and one which is all too commonly ignored in scientific argument (or rhetoric, at any rate); it is clearly stated by Buszkowski (1988a: 92):

Equivalence results on the line categorial-generative grammars ... were sometimes interpreted to shake the value of CGs (as they yield nothing new). The author absolutely disagrees with that standpoint ... that two kinds of grammar are weakly equivalent does not mean, obviously, that they are simply the same. This means, precisely, that they describe the same reality of string-languages. But they describe it in a different way. Categorial description refers to the algebra of types (and, behind it, logical semantics), while phrase-structure description relies upon the algebra of concatentation (or bracketed concatenation). Approximately, categorial grammar theory can be viewed as a logical meta-theory for the theory of phrase-structure grammar.

A number of specific contrasts between the two families can be objectively identified. Bach (1988: 19) expresses the first as between a 'constitutional' and an 'architectural' approach:

> In the former approach, description operates in a primary way by the statement of principles overlaid on some skeleton of a grammar (usually not explicitly given). The primary work goes into stating constraints or licenses. In the architectural approach, of which I consider various categorial theories to be prime examples, the attempt is made to build into the very structure of a grammar various properties from which will follow principles of the sort stipulated independently in the alternative sort of theory.

A nice example in grammatical description is Dowty's argument (1988: 179–82) that various NP-constraints in transformational theory are subsumed by a single constraint on function composition into NP.

At a more abstract level, this 'architectural' nature of CGs appears as the closeness of relations between what other theories may take to be 'autonomous' components of a grammar, most notably that between syntax and semantics discussed above, which is in direct opposition to the Chomskyan principle of the 'autonomy of syntax'.

As noted above, PSGs and CGs are repeatedly contrasted as positional, or configurational, grammars, on the one hand, and functional grammars, on the other. I have already quoted Buszkowski's statement (1988a: 92) that 'Categorial description refers to the algebra of types ... while phrase-structure description relies upon the algebra of concatenation.' The distinction between the tree-theoretic basis of phrase-structure description and the functional basis of categorial description is explicitly discussed by a number of sources, and it is generally argued (if not assumed) that the notion of 'head' should not be primitive, as in Generalized Phrase Structure Grammar (GPSG), but derivative, definable in terms of the more basic notions 'function' and 'argument'.

A final objectively evident contrast of great importance lies in the significance of grammatical categories in CGs and PSGs. The categories of a traditional PSG are atomic and largely arbitrary labels which must be mapped into a separate component of phrase-structure (PS) rules. The categories of a CG are complex objects with a rich information structure, and *replace* PS rules (thus Karttunen's 'radical lexicalism'). This again is remarked on by Buszkowski (1988a: 69): 'From the standpoint of formal linguistics, CGs constitute a refinement of Chomsky's PSGs, since – in opposition to the latter – the former assign an internal structure to category symbols (non-terminals).' As Oehrle (p.c.) comments, 'Phrase structure grammars are very powerful, but not necessarily subtle.' More recent theories of syntax, notably GPSG, use structured categories of various kinds – indeed, this is one of the points of convergence among them – but none go as far as CG in incorporating the whole range of linguistic information in lexical categories.

The contrasts between CGs and PSGs are thus substantive and incontrovertible. Nevertheless, a growing and impressive body of work is distinguished by its constructive eclecticism, its integration of insights from both schools. The clearest example of this is the emergence of Head-driven Phrase Structure Grammar (Pollard 1988; Pollard and Sag 1987), an offshoot of GPSG and Lexical-Functional Grammar (LFG) whose other, equally contributory progenitor is CG. This will be discussed in more detail below, in Chapters 5 and 6.

1.ii PRACTICAL BASICS

So what does it look like; how is it done? I will outline here the most minimal, pure categorial grammar; its extensions will follow in the next two chapters.

I have commented already that it is the categories of a categorial grammar which carry the burden of syntactic, and semantic, description. At the same time, the principle of minimalism requires that no entity, no category is postulated unless it absolutely must be for adequate description of the data. According to CG's foundations in the formal philosophy of language, two and only two types of linguistic entities must exist: bits of language which name entities (therefore called **e**) and bits of language which spell out propositions, which can carry truth-values (and are therefore called **t**). In terms more familiar to theoretical linguistics, the class designating entities is the class of names (**N**), and the truth-bearing class of propositions is the class of declarative sentences (**S**). These are both, in many senses, 'complete', and also irreducible. They thus stand as 'atomic' categories, complete expressions, in any categorial grammar. (Of course, this reductionism is valid from a fairly narrow perspective. Any account of 'situated' language demands a richer ontology, in which spatial and temporal location, identity of speaker and hearer, and so on are also represented. See Ch.4.v and Ch.6.i on the use of Discourse Representation Theory within Unification CG for one attempt to remedy this.)

All other linguistic units are incomplete – 'unsaturated', in the terms of a valency grammar – and need some other expression(s) to occur with them to complete them. They are seen as functions from the expressions they need – their 'arguments' – to the complete expressions then formed, their 'result' or 'value'. (In more logically oriented work, the argument may be called the 'domain', and the value the 'range' of a function.) So, for example, an intransitive verb is a function from a name (*Tigger*) to a sentence (*Tigger complains*), and an adjective, or epithet, is a function from a name to a name (*poor Tigger*). The set of categories is defined recursively: if **X** and **Y** are categories, then a function from **X** to **Y** is also a category. There is no need for **X** and **Y** to be atomic – a transitive verb like *prefer*, to take a simple example, is a function from a name (*fish*) to, effectively, an intransitive verb, a function-from-a-name-to-a-sentence (*prefers fish*; *Tigger prefers fish*). This clearly defines an infinite set, in which categories can grow to arbitrary complexity, a characteristic which – as we will see – has advantages for richness of linguistic description, but problems of formal and computational tractability.

Notice immediately that these are not only syntactic functions but also simultaneously build up a semantic interpretation for a sentence. Both *complains* and *poor* are predicated of *Tigger*, apply to and restrict, refine, its meaning, giving the semantic formulae (simplistically) *poor(Tigger)*, *complains(Tigger)*. This will be discussed much more fully later.

The 'functor categories' or 'complex categories' are most simply written with a vertical 'slash' notation, with the value to the left and the argument to the right of the slash 'connective': the intransitive verb category is **S|N** and the adjective category **N|N**. Parentheses are used in more complex categories to indicate which is the main connective, as in the transitive verb category (**S|N**)**|N**. This is fine for semantic description, but for syntax we need also some way of encoding constraints on word order. Some proposals do use a 'nondirectional' CG even for syntactic description, with word-order constraints given not in the categories but elsewhere (see Ch.6.ii). But most work on syntax uses a 'directional' grammar in which the connective indicates the direction in which the functor must look for its argument. The vertical slash is replaced (or supplemented) by two directional slashes, a forward slash / when the argument must come to the right of the functor and a backslash \ when the argument must come to the left. The intransitive verb category is now **S\N**, a function from a preceding name to a sentence, accepting *Tigger complains* but not **complains Tigger* as a grammatical sentence. An English adjective is **N/N**, as its noun must follow it; a transitive verb is **(S\N)/N**, followed by its object and preceded by its subject. (The exact form of even this simple notation is unfortunately a vexed current issue, to be discussed briefly in the next section, Ch.1.iii.)

This gives us a way of describing the syntactic (and parallel semantic) behaviour of any word by means of its category, which is assigned to it in the lexicon. Any word with a number of different behaviour patterns will correspondingly have a number of different categories, so that a verb like *eat*, which can be either transitive or intransitive (*Tigger eats doves*; *Tigger eats*) will have the two categories **(S\N)/N**, **S\N**. There is no one category corresponding to 'verb'. A categorial lexicon is therefore in one sense larger than is typical of other linguistic theories, but that is a symptom of the centrality of the lexicon rather than of any greater overall complexity of the grammar as a whole. More important is the lack of any simple way to express generalizations about inflection, complementation patterns and the like. Notations have been suggested for a generalized 'verb' category, which would not be assigned to lexical items, but could be used in, for example, morphological rules, to denote the appropriate set of lexical categories. 'Lexical rules' can be used to state common alternations in complementation, the optionality of particular arguments, and so on. However, these possibilities have not been thoroughly explored, and this must be recognized as an area in which CGs could be strengthened.

Given a lexicon full of atomic and complex category assignments, it is possible to identify the categories of the individual words in a sentence; but to check the legality of that sentence and derive a semantic interpretation there must be rules which can be applied to those categories. As the complex categories are functors, the basic operation involved is application of each functor to its argument. Schematically, **X/Y Y → X**, a functor looking forward for a **Y** to form **X**, followed by a **Y**, combine to form an **X**. Similarly, a backward-looking functor preceded by its argument will combine to give the specified value,

Y X\Y → X. The process is very much like the cancellation of fractions, with the value as numerator and argument as denominator in the functor category, and its application to its argument working like multiplication − this is clearer in the 'vertical' notation used by Ajdukiewicz (1935), where the value is written above, rather than before, the argument (see below, Ch.1.iii). As the categories are combined and the string reduced towards **S**, its semantic interpretation is built up by the same process of function application. (This basic combination rule, and others used in richer categorial systems, will be discussed more fully in the next chapter.)

In the notation most commonly used for derivations, the string of categories is set out, and each operation of application is indicated by underlining the functor and its argument, indexing the underline with the rule used and its direction, and giving the resulting value below the underline. (The semantic interpretation is by no means always given, especially for simple cases.)

1.1 Tigger complains

$$\underline{\begin{matrix} \text{N} & \text{S\textbackslash N} \end{matrix}}_{<A}$$
$$\text{S} \qquad\qquad complains(Tigger)$$

1.2 Tigger eats doves

$$\text{N} \quad \underline{\begin{matrix} \text{(S\textbackslash N)/N} & \text{N} \end{matrix}}_{>A}$$
$$\underline{\qquad\quad \text{S\textbackslash N} \qquad\quad}_{<A} \quad eats(doves)$$
$$\text{S} \qquad\qquad (eats(doves))(Tigger)$$

The pattern of derivation shown by the underlines has the same structure as a conventional phrase-structure tree for these sentences (as it generally does for this simple CG, although not for the richer ones), but notice that no syntactic structure is produced. The string of categories is progressively reduced towards **S**, with the semantic interpretation developed at each step, but there is no level of syntactic analysis as such. Some recent, especially computational, work holds a record of the derivational history for a sentence to serve any purposes for which a syntactic structure might be useful, but that is in no way essential. To quote Moortgat (1988b: 60), 'The level of autonomous syntax turns out to be a dispensable artefact between the two indispensable levels of sound and meaning.'

Atomic and functional categories related by function application form the heart of any categorial grammar. There are many extensions to this core, a few to the set of atomic categories and a great many to the set of rules, some very widely accepted and others idiosyncratic. The rules of the 'classical' extended CG defined by Lambek (1958) are set out in more detail in Chapter 3, and some of the later, less standard proposals in Chapter 4.

1.iii NOTATIONAL VARIANTS

Before going on to more interesting things, however, it is necessary to clarify the issue of notation. A number of different notations have been used for complex categories even in classical CGs in the past, and indeed still are. These are, of course, all formally equivalent, and should be 'mere notational variants' if any variants are, but require some explanation to avoid confusion. In fact, they have interestingly different powers of suggestion, and each has vociferous proponents.

Many of the early Polish logicians did – and some still do, see Marciszewski (1988), especially pages 18–19 on 'Terminological and notational variants' – use a colon : as their only connective, infixed between value and argument, or prefixed to all of them as in 'Polish notation' for formal languages. (As their concern is entirely with semantics, there is no need for any indication of word order, and indeed the first stage of any derivation in this style is to re-order the category string so that all functors precede their arguments.)

The linguist is unlikely to meet this notation, except perhaps in Geach (1972), where it is adequately explained, so I shall not consider it further. Another rather different format, that of Categorial Unification Grammars, is discussed below (Ch.4.v), and meanwhile does not lead to any risk of confusion.

In the logical and Montagovian traditions it remains common, as for example in the work of Partee and van Benthem, to use **e** and **t** as atomic categories, and to write (non-directional) functor categories in angle brackets, argument before result: thus a predicate is of category $\langle e,t \rangle$ (a function from an entity to a truth-value) and a transitive verb takes two entities to a truth-value, $\langle e,\langle e,t \rangle \rangle$. There remain three versions of the fractional notation, associated primarily with the work of Ajdukiewicz, Lambek and Steedman.

In Ajdukiewicz's original (1935) notation (followed by Lyons 1971; Flynn 1983), complex categories are written vertically, result over argument, a form which is clear and unambiguous but can eat up space on the page – the category of a modifier of adverbs (a function from an adverb to an adverb, where an adverb is a function from a predicate to a predicate, where a predicate is a function from a name to a sentence), such as *very* in Ajdukiewicz's example sentence *The lilac smells very strongly* ..., is

$$\cfrac{\cfrac{\cfrac{\dfrac{s}{n}}{\dfrac{s}{n}}}{\dfrac{s}{n}}}{\dfrac{s}{n}}$$

(Ajdukiewicz 1935: 211)

It therefore soon became customary to write complex categories horizontally, with a diagonal slash, as we have seen, replacing the original horizontal divider. This notation exists in two distinct forms. Both, in a directional CG, use the direction of the diagonal 'slash' operator to encode restrictions on word order, a 'forwards' slash / indicating that the function takes its argument on the right, a 'back-slash' \ looking to the left. The directional systems of Lambek (1958, 1987) and Bar-Hillel (1960) approximate the original fractional nota-tion by writing the result on top of the slash, as it were, and the argu-ment underneath. As the direction of the slash varies to indicate the relative order of functor and argument, the order of elements in the complex category symbol varies correspondingly, the argument element consistently lying adjacent to the argument itself in a gram-matical sequence. The remaining alternative is the one I have used on pp. 9–10, in which the value is always written to the left and the argu-ment to the right, regardless of the direction of the slash. This is used in many non-directional systems, and thus originally more often when the focus was on semantics than syntax. It is adopted in the non-directional syntactic category system of Ades and Steedman (1982), and first suggested in a directional system, it seems, independently around 1985 by Dowty (published as Dowty 1988) and Steedman (published as Steedman 1987) (Steedman, p.c.).

The three notations can be most readily compared by setting out a few complex categories and both forms of the application rule in all three together (Table 1.1). The Ajdukiewicz notation is unambiguous; categories in the other two are marked (adapting a suggestion from

Table 1.1 Categorial notations compared

	Ajdukiewicz	Lambek	Steedman
Complex categories:	$\dfrac{\text{result}}{\text{argument}}$	$res/arg_L,\ arg\backslash res_L$	$res/arg_S,\ res\backslash arg_S$
Intransitive verb:	$\dfrac{s}{n}$	$N\backslash S_L$	$S\backslash N_S$
Adjective:	$\dfrac{n}{n}$	N/N_L	N/N_S
Transitive verb:	$\dfrac{\frac{s}{n}}{n}$	$(N\backslash S)/N_L$	$(S\backslash N)/N_S$

Function application, forwards (FA) and backwards (BA):

FA:	$\dfrac{a}{b}\ b \rightarrow a$	$A/B_L\ B \rightarrow A$	$A/B_S\ B \rightarrow A$
BA:	$b\ \dfrac{a}{b} \rightarrow a$	$B\ B\backslash A_L \rightarrow A$	$B\ A\backslash B_S \rightarrow A$

Oehrle) with a subscript indicating which form of the notation they use.

Lambek defends his notation (Lambek 1987) on the grounds that only adjacent terms cancel, as just shown; that for every valid formula the mirror-image is also a valid formula; and, in particular, that type-raisings (to be explained later, Ch.3.iv) appear in symmetric pairs. Certainly, a number of rules are most perspicuous in this notation, especially the symmetry of those with both forward and backward forms. However, for complex categories with multiple slashes of both directions it is not obvious – at least to a human processor and on first glance – what is to be the immediate argument or the final output. There is also no obvious way of encoding either a neutral or an infix slash connective.

Steedman's system maintains transparency of result and argument – the 'leading edge' or first element in any complex category will always be its final output, the final element its immediate input. It is also appropriate for head-initial languages, where arguments do occur to the right of their functors, and for incremental processing in general. It does have the drawback that backward rules, especially the more complex ones such as backward composition (Ch.3.iii), are not immediately obvious, and the symmetry between the backward and forward forms is obscured totally.

At present the original, Lambek notation ('result on top') seems to be the most commonly used in mainland Europe, 'result first' in Britain and the United States; from another viewpoint, but not entirely coincidentally, 'result on top' is more often used by those working on formal and logical properties of CGs, 'result first' by those concentrating on the description of linguistic data. (These are, of course, crude generalizations, and there are exceptions.) I have chosen the latter here, partly because this introduction is aimed more at linguists than logicians, partly because it is the form I myself (as a linguist) have always used, and regularly think in. I have used Lambek notation in parallel where it seemed the clearer of the two, and in quotations the notation of the original has been preserved or minimally adapted, with glosses or translations where that seemed helpful.

FURTHER READING

There has been no easily accessible introduction to categorial grammars – each new paper or thesis has restated the basics in its first few pages, but there has been nothing really appropriate for, say, an undergraduate reading list. Curry (1961) introduces the underlying logical principles. Lyons (1971: 227–31) is a clear statement of the most elementary principles and notation, but in terms of (a simplified) Montague semantics, and not obviously of great interest to the ordinary working grammarian. Lewis (1972) goes further, but along the same lines. Lambek (1958) is a lucid, linguistically significant discussion of the algebra, virtually unobtainable until its recent re-issue in Buszkowski *et al.* (1988). Many of Steedman's papers begin with good linguistically oriented introductions, especially Ades and Steedman (1982), which is probably the best starting point for most linguists. The editors' introduction to Oehrle *et al.* (1988) is somewhat advanced and formalist, the set of introductions to Buszkowski *et al.* (1988) even more so, but Bach (1988) is a fine basic statement of the motivating principles of the enterprise.

2 A brief history

Categorial grammars, as I have already suggested, have a long and distinguished history, but one which is quite distinct from the background to phrase-structure grammars, and unfamiliar to many linguists. They are rooted in the mathematical logic of Frege (1879, 1891, 1892) and Ajdukiewicz (1935), developing in two independent and very different streams through early work in computational treatments of syntax by Bar-Hillel (1953) and in formal semantics by Richard Montague (Thomason 1974b), and finding an explosive very recent productivity most clearly initiated by the fusion of logic, computation, syntax and semantics in Ades and Steedman (1982). It is worth outlining this background, as it will be helpful in understanding the concerns and concepts of the theory as it now stands.

2.i THE EVOLUTION OF LINGUISTIC THEORY

We are accustomed today to hearing linguistics described as a science, and conducted like one; and, of course, explicitness and precision have been desiderata in linguistic description for thousands of years. The exact nature or emphasis of that endeavour has, however, changed significantly through time. This development is nicely summarized by Winograd (1983: 6–13) with a series of metaphors.

1 *Linguistics as law.* Prescriptive grammar – not a phase in the evolution of linguistics, but a distinct and continuing tradition – is concerned to stipulate and circumscribe the 'correct' use of language. This is the way grammar is standardly taught in schools, but is, of course, quite contrary to the means and ends of descriptive linguistics of any variety.

2 *Linguistics as biology.* Comparative grammar, especially comparative

philology, dominated language studies in the nineteenth century. The theory of evolution influenced linguistics, as it did other sciences; family relationships among languages were seen to be analogous to those among plant and animal species, language taxonomies were established and common-ancestor languages reconstructed.

3 *Linguistics as chemistry.* Starting with the teaching of de Saussure at the beginning of the twentieth century, and gathering real momentum since the 1930s with the work of Bloomfield and his followers, there was a shift of emphasis from the relations between languages, often seen primarily diachronically, to the internal, synchronic structures of individual languages. Structural (descriptive) linguistics aimed to identify the constituent elements of a language and the patterns in which they combine to form larger units, words forming sentences, morphemes words, and phonemes morphemes:

> The analysis of language data was modelled after a positivist view of the empirical sciences that emphasized the use of experimental techniques to rigorously determine underlying structure. A chemist performs experiments to determine the set of molecules of which a complex substance is composed, and in turn analyzes those molecules in terms of their basic elements. The great success of chemistry was in finding a small set of primitive elements whose combinations could account for the vast number of different substances found in nature. Language, with its sentences, made up of words, made up of sounds, was subject to the same kind of analysis.
>
> (Winograd 1983: 10–11)

2.ii ORIGINS OF THE FORMALIST ENTERPRISE

Winograd's fourth metaphor is that of linguistics as mathematics, characterizing the generative enterprise. Here the focus shifts from the empirically observed surface forms of language to its abstract, formal underlying grammar.

> Generative linguistics views language as a mathematical object and builds theories that are very much like sets of axioms and inference rules in mathematics. A sentence is grammatical if there is some derivation that demonstrates that its structure is in

accord with the set of rules, much as a proof demonstrates the
truth of a mathematical sentence.

(1983: 12)

Current logic-based computational models of 'parsing as deduction',
such as the 'Lambek theorem proving' approach of Moortgat (1988b),
and the algebraic strand in categorial grammars, make this more than
an illustrative analogy.

The credit for initiating this metaphor, or paradigm, shift is generally given to Chomsky's (1957) *Syntactic Structures*, but the convergence of linguistics and mathematics is clearly evident in even the titles
of Frege's (1879) 'Begriffsschrift, eine der arithmetischen nachgebil-
dete Formelsprache des reinen Denkens' (*'Begriffsschrift*, a formula
language, modelled upon that of arithmetic, for pure thought'),
Bar-Hillel's (1953) 'A quasi-arithmetical notation for syntactic
description' and Lambek's (1958) 'The mathematics of sentence structure', three seminal papers for categorial linguistics. For influence on
the linguistic community at large, however, *Syntactic Structures* must
be admitted to stand unparalleled. The distinguishing of various levels
of linguistic description, the related concepts of kernel sentences and
of transformations, the divorce of semantics from syntax all found
widespread support and have (directly or through their lineal descen-
dants) profoundly coloured most linguistic theory of the past thirty
years.

It has been left for computational linguistics to take up the explicit
location of natural language grammars within formal language theory
which Chomsky begins to explore in the chapter on 'An elementary
linguistic theory', (Chomsky 1957: 18–25), where a proof is presented
of the inadequacy of any finite state Markov process for the description of English. The exploration is taken further in Chomsky and
Miller's (1963) 'Introduction to the formal analysis of natural
languages', in the *Handbook of Mathematical Psychology*. For
Chomsky and Miller,

the (finite) set of rules specifying a particular language constitutes the grammar of that language ... a grammar must have the
status of a theory about those recurrent regularities that we call
the syntactic structure of the language. To the extent that a
grammar is formalized, it constitutes a mathematical theory of
the syntactic structure of a particular natural language.

(1963: 285)

The details of their account, and of Chomsky's (1963) 'Formal properties of grammars' in the same volume, need not be rehearsed here. It is interesting, however, to note in the latter a concluding section (1963: 410–14) on categorial grammars, sketching Bar-Hillel's bidirectional system (see Ch.2.iii.b below), 'a precise explication of the immediate constituent analysis of recent linguistics' (ibid.: 411). Chomsky observes that 'The interest of the various kinds of categorial grammars is that they contain no grammatical rules beyond the lexicon' (ibid.: 413), but doubts their usefulness for real linguistic description:

> for those subparts of actual languages that can be described in a fairly natural way by context-free grammars, a corresponding description in terms of bidirectional categorial systems becomes complex fairly rapidly (and, of course [*sic*], a natural description with a unidirectional categorial grammar is generally quite out of the question).
>
> (ibid.)

This is the closest he gets to an actual argument against categorial grammars, the mood of this four-page tailpiece to a hundred-page paper being less one of reasoned consideration than of dismissal. (Chomsky (1965: 124ff. and fn. 34) contains a similarly dismissive reference to Curry and Šaumjan, which we will return to below, Ch.6.ii.)

2.iii ORIGINS OF CATEGORIAL GRAMMAR

2.iii.a Mathematics

The first serious and detailed categorial syntax for natural language is the fragment presented in Bar-Hillel's (1953) 'A quasi-arithmetical notation for syntactic description'. The insight which motivated and informed that paper (which will be discussed below, Ch.2.iii.b) was the potential of 'combin[ing] methods developed by the Polish logician Kasimir Ajdukiewicz on the one hand and by American structural linguists [e.g. Harris, Fries] on the other' (1953: 61). The attractions of this method of syntactic description were its economy and precision:

> only a simple rule of a quasi-arithmetical character need be given to enable us to 'compute' the syntactic character of any given

linguistic string. ... This should be of value in those situations
in which a completely mechanical procedure is required.

(ibid.)

This 'quasi-arithmetical' nature of categorial grammars, adduced in
their favour by Bar-Hillel *en passant*, can be traced directly to the
work of Gottlob Frege, who first extended the concept of a function
in mathematics to mathematical logic and thence to natural language.
Frege's (1879) *Begriffsschrift* ('ideography' or 'concept writing'),
among a number of fundamental contributions to logic, first suggested the analysis of propositions into function and argument rather
than subject and predicate:

> If in an expression ... a simple or a compound sign has one or
> more occurrences and if we regard that sign as replaceable in all
> or some of these occurrences by something else (but everywhere
> by the same thing), then we call the part that remains invariant
> in the expression a function, and the replaceable part the
> argument of the function.

(1879: 22)

An expression can be analysed by a number of different func-
tion/argument relations, depending on which elements are held constant and which are altered, as for the example *Cato killed Cato*:

> If we here think of 'Cato' as replaceable at its first occurrence,
> 'to kill Cato' is the function; if we think of 'Cato' as replaceable
> at its second occurrence, 'to be killed by Cato' is the function;
> if, finally, we think of 'Cato' as replaceable at both occurrences,
> then 'to kill oneself' is the function.

(ibid.)

The expression of these relations in natural language is similarly
flexible:

> In the mind of the speaker the subject is ordinarily the main
> argument; the next in importance often appears as the object.
> Through the choice between [grammatical] forms, such as
> active–passive, or between words, such as 'heavier'–'lighter'
> and 'give'–'receive', ordinary language is free to allow this or
> that component of the sentence to appear as main argument at

will, a freedom that, however, is restricted by the scarcity of words.

(1879: 23)

The proposal is developed a little further in 'Funktion und Begriff' (1891). Most of that paper again concerns mathematical logic, but one brief paragraph deserves quotation in full:

> Statements in general, just like equations or inequalities or expressions in Analysis, can be imagined to be split up into two parts; one complete in itself, and the other in need of supplementation, or 'unsaturated'. Thus, e.g., we split up the sentence
>
>   *Caesar conquered Gaul*
>
> into *Caesar* and *conquered Gaul*. The second part is 'unsaturated' — it contains an empty place; only when this place is filled up with a proper name, does a complete sense appear. Here too I give the name 'function' to what this 'unsaturated' part stands for. In this case the argument is *Caesar*.

(1891: 31)

The importance of Frege's work to the development of logic is stressed by Potts (1988: 238); both his points are of continuing relevance to categorial linguistics:

> It is to Frege's grammar that we owe the two most definitive advances in logic since the end of the middle ages. First, it allows us to analyze propositions in more than one way. ... Second, [it] distinguish[es] between functors of second-level and expressions of basic categories.

One should mention also the work of later mathematical logicians, notably Curry (1930, 1961) and Schönfinkel (1924), which continues to influence the development of categorial grammars (see, for example, the recent use of combinators by Steedman and others, discussed below (Ch.4.iii)).

These crucial suggestions were developed far more fully by Joachim Lambek in his 1958 paper 'The mathematics of sentence structure'. This appeared in the *American Mathematical Monthly*, 'addressed to mathematicians with at most an amateur interest in linguistics', which may explain its lack of currency among linguists; it has now been reprinted in Buszkowski *et al.* (1988: 153–72) (from which I take the pagination). Its opening (reminiscent of the much better known opening of Montague's 'Universal grammar', quoted below, Ch.2.iii.c) states that

> The aim of this paper is to obtain an effective rule (or algorithm) for distinguishing sentences from nonsentences, which works not only for the formal languages of interest to the mathematical logician, but also for natural languages such as English, or at least for fragments of such languages.
>
> (1958 [1988]: 153)

After an introduction to 'the theory of syntactic types', Lambek turns to

> a development of the technique of Ajdukiewicz and Bar-Hillel in a mathematical direction. We introduce a calculus of types, which is related to the well-known calculus of residuals. (Footnote: The calculus presented here is formally identical with a calculus constructed … for a discussion of canonical mappings in linear and multilinear algebra.)
>
> (ibid.: 154)

The details of this calculus will be discussed fully below (Ch.3). The point to be made here is that Lambek offers a fusion of mathematics and linguistics, one calculus applying both to formal algebra and to natural language, explicit in both principle and detail. This insight and objective – the possibility of a mathematics of language, the vision of syntax as algebra – is fundamental to the categorial enterprise.

2.iii.b Natural language syntax

The linguistically motivated development of simple categorial grammars for the direct description of natural language syntax had been taken up earlier, in the work of Yehoshua Bar-Hillel in the 1950s. His major insight was the compatibility of the compositional models of semantic interpretation developed by Ajdukiewicz and others with the syntactic descriptions of natural language then current among American structuralists such as Fries and Zellig Harris. The impetus came from the earliest American attempts at machine translation, to which Bar-Hillel was first an active and influential contributor, later a disillusioned opponent.

Electronic digital computers had given a hint of their potential during the Second World War, when their use in cryptanalysis had been vital to both American and British operations. After the war, this led Warren Weaver to circulate a now famous memorandum suggesting that the techniques developed for code-breaking might also be appropriate for machine translation between natural languages. The ensuing rush of research funds and interest was largely responsible, in Bar-Hillel's opinion, for the sudden rise of structuralist linguistics in the early 1950s, especially 'its special offspring to deal with mechanical structure determination, i.e., algebraic linguistics, also called, when this application is particularly stressed, computational linguistics' (Bar-Hillel 1962: 186–7).

If structuralist linguistics was already serviceable for the computational analysis of language, Bar-Hillel saw clearly that categorial grammar could be even more so. Like the structuralist model, it would establish the immediate constituent structure of a sentence (he later (Bar-Hillel *et al.* 1960: 103) described it as 'meant to be a precise explicatum of the notion of immediate constituent grammar', in contrast to the view which takes it to be a dependency grammar), but it had the great advantage, for computation, of being simpler and easier to calculate, requiring only a lexicon and a simple rule of combination by 'arithmetical multiplication of fractions', without any 'special syntactic statements' (Bar-Hillel 1953: 61). This one operation of fraction cancellation finds both the connexity of a string and its constituents.

To do this for natural language, however, the model needed a certain amount of modification. Ajdukiewicz had been concerned with the semantics of formal languages, free of ambiguity, and written in Polish notation, a positional formalism which, rather than grouping by parentheses, places operators always immediately to the left of their arguments; it is thus a unidirectional categorial grammar. Bar-Hillel added the necessary possibility of category ambiguity, that is, of a word belonging to more than one category. He also added backwards operators and backwards cancellation, allowing an operator to take its argument from the left or the right: in other words, he was the first to propose a bidirectional CG, making possible the use of more 'intuitively natural-looking category assignments' (Bar-Hillel *et al.* 1960: 101–2) than in a unidirectional CG. He can thus produce derivations like 2.1, for example (Bar-Hillel 1953: 63; arguments in square brackets are to be looked for on the right of the functor, those in parentheses on the left):

2.1 John	knew	that	Paul	was	a	poor	man
n	s/(n)[n]	n/[s]	n	s/(n)[n]	n/[n]	n/[n]	n
n	s/(n)[n]	n/[s]	n	s/(n)[n]	n/[n]	n	
n	s/(n)[n]	n/[s]	n	s/(n)[n]	n		
n	s/(n)[n]	n/[s]	s				
n	s/(n)[n]	n					
s							

One central concept in structuralist linguistics which Bar-Hillel's work proves to be unimportant is that of constituenthood. Within a legal string, a substring is 'connex', that is, a constituent, under a particular derivation if at some point in that derivation it is labelled by a single category.

> It makes a considerable difference in the organization of immediate and other constituents whether we treat *loves* (say) as an operator which out of a left **n** *John* and a right **n** *Mary* forms a sentence, *John loves Mary*, IN ONE COMPLEX STEP, or as an operator which out of a right **n** *Mary* forms an operator, *loves Mary*, which out of a left **n** *John* forms a sentence IN TWO SIMPLE STEPS. According to the second treatment, *loves Mary* is an immediate constituent of the whole; according to the first, it is no constituent at all. The fact that being-a-constituent-of is a relation which is not invariant even with respect to such 'inessential' transformations ... shows that this relation and its cognates are of somewhat restricted importance.
>
> (ibid.: 70)

With hindsight, this foreshadows the 'flexibility' of extended CGs. At the time, its relation to formal logics was more obvious: Bar-Hillel mentions the work of Curry (1950) comparing the use of 'singulary operators with complex numerators' with 'n-ary operators with simple denominators' (ibid.: 71), an issue which will also arise again (e.g. Ch.4.ii.d).

By 1960, however, Bar-Hillel was less optimistic about the adequacy of his categorial grammar. His doubts arose mainly from its inability to deal with discontinuous constituents – troublesome for any grammar which eschews movement rules, and a major focus of current work (see Ch. 5.iii.c). Thus, for example, he points out, one could not derive *He looked it up*, on the natural reading which takes *up* to be of category **n\s\\(n\s)/n** ('an operator that out of an intransitive verbal to its left forms a transitive verbal' (1960: 82); note this is Lambek notation, and the double slash indicates the 'principal' connective, just as parentheses do − **((s\n)/n)\(s\n)** is the result-first equivalent), and *looked up* to be a constituent. One might object to this type assignment, since not all intransitive verbs can be transitivized by *up*, but the inflexibility of word order will remain a problem. Similarly, sentences with infixed sentential adverbials, such as *John, unfortunately, was asleep* cannot be derived as grammatical, which, of course, they are.

These deficiencies in a simple CG are exactly those which characterize an immediate-constituent grammar (see the discussion of the latter in Chomsky and Miller 1963: 297ff.), and follow from the provable weak equivalence of such a CG with a simple context-free phrase-structure grammar. Bar-Hillel was well aware of this, and indeed responsible, with his associates in Israel, for producing the proof (Bar-Hillel *et al.* 1960). The need for some extension of the basic grammar was clear to him. At the time, and for some time afterwards, the transformational model seemed the obvious means for this. Bar-Hillel did comment on Lambek's much richer calculus (Bar-Hillel 1960: 83), but believed that its greater complexity could at best improve efficiency in parsing: 'The situation is apparently not changed very much ... it is not clear whether Lambek's model is really more powerful than the one outlined above [see pp. 22–3, this volume]' (ibid.).

Bar-Hillel's work is not always appreciated, partly, perhaps, due to its involvement with the practical (and for a long time intellectually discredited) task of machine translation, partly to its relatively early date (from the prevailing current perspective) and its abandonment, even by its author. He was the first to apply the categorial model to a reasonably wide range of syntactic phenomena in natural language, to confront its shortcomings and to consider seriously and explicitly, in detail, what modifications and extensions it might need for fuller linguistic coverage. But categorial syntax died with Bar-Hillel's interest in it, and was reborn only as a separate branch from the semantic stem.

A separate, but clearly similar enterprise has been steadily pursued since the early 1960s in Russia by Šaumjan and his colleagues, under the name of 'applicative grammar' (see, for example, Šaumjan 1973; Soboleva 1973). They distinguish an abstract, universal 'genotype grammar' from the specific grammars of actual languages, the 'phenotype grammars'. There are three fundamental classes of linguistic objects: the names of objects (terms), the names of situations (sentences) and 'transformers' which can form one from another exactly as do functor categories in a CG. Rigorous formal proofs of validity are applied to a wide range of syntactic and morphological data, most of it Russian. It is regrettable that the language barrier has kept this work from wider currency in the west.

2.iii.c Formal semantics

The semantic ancestry of categorial grammars is even older. Traceable in general terms to Aristotle, and in quite specific ways to Frege and to Edmund Husserl, it continues through a distinguished line whose most outstanding members are Kazimierz Ajdukiewicz and Richard Montague.

Frege's informing contributions to the categorial enterprise are his extension of the concept of a function in mathematics to mathematical logic and thence to natural language, discussed above, and his eponymous principle of semantic compositionality, commonly paraphrased as 'The meaning of the whole is a function of the meaning of the parts and their mode of combination.' This one is harder to place, but something like it permeates much of Frege's extensive study of meaning, as in the discussion of the contribution made to the sense and reference of a sentence by the sense and possible lack of reference of a part of it, in 'Über Sinn und Bedeutung' (1892).

The Fourth Investigation of Husserl's *Logische Untersuchungen* (1900), titled 'The distinction between independent and non-independent meanings and the idea of pure grammar', sets out various aspects of his *Bedeutungskategorien* ('meaning categories'). The distinctions which he says must be kept clear in discussing meaning include that between simple and complex, and between independent ('categorematic') and non-independent ('syncategorematic') expressions. 'Pure grammar' has as its task to

1 assign meaning categories to the expressions of language;
2 specify which combinations of meaning categories are possible;
3 state the laws that regulate the combination of meaning categories.

This was the basis for the logic developed by Leśniewski and Ajdukiewicz in Poland in the 1920s and 1930s. Ajdukiewicz's 1935 paper 'Die syntaktische Konnexität' is generally acknowledged to be the single most important seminal work in the development of categorial grammar. The system presented there is primarily designed for the analysis of formal (logical) languages. This is evident in his use of only two basic categories, **s** (sentence) and **n** (name), despite his own discussion (1935: 209–10) of the apparent need for distinct categories for 'singular' and 'general' names in 'ordinary' language and of the possibilities of cross-linguistic variation in the category set; in his extensive treatment of the distinction between functors and operators; and in his re-ordering of categories into their 'proper index sequence' before derivation begins.

However, we find here also the first explicit application of a categorial system to natural language analysis. It is Ajdukiewicz who first makes the distinction between basic categories and functor categories (attributing the latter to Kotarbinski), who first uses a fractional notation for functors, who first discusses the adequacy of such a system for 'ordinary' language, and who first offers a categorial derivation for a sentence of such a language (1935: 215–16):

```
2.2  Der   Flieder  duftet  sehr    stark    und   die  Rose  blüht
    (The   lilac    smells  very    strongly and   the  rose  blooms)

      n       n        s      s        s       s     n    n     s
      ─                ─      ─        ─        ─     ─          ─
      n                n      n        n        ss    n          n
                              ─        ─
                              s        s
                              ─        ─
                              n        n
                              ─
                              s
                              ─
                              n
                              ─
                              s
                              ─
                              n
```

The 'proper index sequence' places every functor in front of its arguments, in the format of Polish notation:

```
2.3          s
             ─
             n
             ─
             s        s
             ─        ─
    s        n        n    s   n   n   s   n   n
    ─        ─        ─
    ss       s        s    n   n       n   n
             ─        ─
             n        n
             ─
             s
             ─
             n
```

Successive fraction cancellations, or function applications, reduce this sequence to the 'final derivative', or 'exponent', **s**.

It is in this logical tradition that one should place a remarkable proposal for categorial syntax, Peter Geach's (1972) 'A program for syntax'. Drawing his inspiration from Ajdukiewicz and the other Polish logicians, Geach sketches an account of verbs, conjunctions, adverbs, prepositions and relative pronouns. One particularly interesting point is his exploration of recursive rules of category division, for example in describing alternative scopes for negation (see Ch.3.v) and the structure of 'right node raising' (see Ch.5.iii.d): thence one form is commonly known as 'the Geach rule'. The paper is notable, and exciting, for the range of insights, formal, semantic and syntactic, it compresses into a short programmatic statement, and rightly has had an influence on CG out of all proportion to its length.

The other great figure in this semantic line is Richard Montague, whose tragically few contributions to the field combine breadth and ambition with formal precision and detail. It is worth repeating here the well-known opening of his (1970) paper 'Universal grammar':

There is in my opinion no important theoretical difference between natural languages and the artificial languages of logicians; indeed, I consider it possible to comprehend the syntax and semantics of both kinds of languages within a single natural and mathematically precise theory.

(1970: 222)

A footnote which follows very shortly after comments that 'I fail to see any great interest in syntax except as a preliminary to semantics' (ibid.: 223), a view with which many categorial grammarians, even those working on syntax, will have some sympathy.

This paper and its (1973) successor, 'The proper treatment of quantification in ordinary English' ('PTQ'; cited as deriving from work as early as 1966), have been enormously influential for both logicians and linguists. Ajdukiewicz's proposals for the analysis of logical languages are developed into a rich formal semantics for natural languages.

The system of 'PTQ' uses two semantic primitives, **e** and **t**, 'the categories of entity expressions (or individual expressions) and truth value expressions (or declarative sentences) respectively' (Montague 1973: 249). These or their combinations are mapped to nine 'traditional syntactic categories', of which five are given 'special symbols'. **N** and **S**, the direct syntactic analogues of **e** and **t**, are not included. The set is given in Table 2.1.

Semantics is the primary concern here, imposing its shape on

Table 2.1 The category system of Montague's PTQ

Syntactic category	Abbreviation	Explanation	Example from the lexicon	Alternative notation
e		entity expression		N
t		truth-value expression		S
t/e	IV	verb phrase or intransitive verb	*run*	S/N
t/IV	T	term	*John, he*	S/(S/N)

(A term phrase does not just refer to an entity, but to an entity with a specific role, as a function from a verb phrase to a full proposition. This is the type commonly assigned to subjects by 'raising' – see Ch.3.iv below.)

IV/T	TV	transitive verb	*find*	(S/N)/(S/(S/N))
IV/IV	IAV	verb phrase modifier	*rapidly*	(S/N)/(S/N)
t/e	CN	common noun	*man*	S/N

(The double slash here differentiates this category from the category t/e of intransitive verbs; common nouns are also taken to be functions from entities to propositions.)

t/t		sentential adverb	*necessarily*	S/S
IAV/T		preposition	*in*	((S/N)/(S/N))/(S/(S/N))

(This, of course, only describes prepositional phrases as verb phrase modifiers.)

IV/t		verb taking a sentential complement	*believe that*	(S/N)/S
IV/IV		verb taking an infinitival complement	*try to*	(S/N)/(S/N)

Source: Montague 1973: 249–50

syntax. The data are those of the logician rather than the linguist: quantification scope and *de dicto/de re* ambiguities, intensional and extensional verbs. But it is the semantics and syntax of natural language *per se*, and (even in the compass of only a few short papers) no mere programmatic sketch but a well-articulated, detailed proposal.

The technicalities of Montagovian model-theoretic semantics lie beyond my present scope (the interested reader is referred to Dowty *et al.* 1981). But it is worth pointing out the distinction between Montague semantics and the analogous syntactic model. The semantic system has had a crucial influence on many current formalist grammars, including Lexical-Functional Grammar and Generalized Phrase Structure Grammar, which reject categorial syntax, while the syntactic system has at least in part broken free and can be found mapped to a number of semantic alternatives, notably the combinatory systems of Steedman, Szabolcsi and Wittenburg. Some of this will be discussed later (Ch.6.i).

2.iv SYNTHESIS AND RENAISSANCE

It was Montague's semantics, not the earlier attempts at categorial syntactic description, which inspired the growth of 'Montague Grammar' through the 1970s. The people involved had evenly balanced backgrounds in philosophy and/or linguistics, and their objective was, correspondingly, a more even balance of semantics and syntax in linguistic description than had been attained before (although still clearly semantics-driven).

Montague's collected papers, edited by Richmond Thomason, were published in 1974; Barbara Partee's 'Montague grammar and transformational grammar', which appeared in *Linguistic Inquiry* the following year (Partee 1975), is a crucial milestone in the development of these ideas, and her (1976) collection *Montague Grammar* remains the essential reference. The contributors to that volume, both linguists and philosophers, from their different perspectives, 'all share with Montague a concern for treating semantics as rigorously as syntax and a desire to uncover systematic connections between the two' (Partee 1976: xi). At the time, this was distinctive, even startling: the overwhelmingly dominant research paradigm for linguistics was Chomsky's transformational model, in which syntax was proclaimed to be autonomous and formal semantics was despaired of.

This profound difference in foundational principles between the two approaches should be kept firmly in mind when looking at some of the more transformational-ish extensions which were proposed for

Montague Grammar. Partee, for example, in the significantly titled (1973) 'Some transformational extensions of Montague Grammar', adds to the basic framework labelled bracketing, to disambiguate $_{IV}[_{IV}[try\ to\ _{IV}[walk]]\ and\ _{IV}[talk]]$ vs $_{IV}[try\ to\ _{IV}[_{IV}[walk]\ and\ _{IV}[talk]]]$ (1973: 64), and a 'starred variable convention' to deal with pronouns in derived verb phrases. She offers rules for reflexivization, passivization, passive agent deletion, tough-movement, subject-raising and object-raising, 'in essentially their classical forms' (ibid.: 65), but with the corresponding explicitly formalized semantic translation rule given as part of each. The first non-transformational syntactic analysis is Thomason's (1974a) account of complement constructions in a Montague framework. However, Emmon Bach (1979a), in a comparable spirit to Partee, presents a grammar comparable to that of 'PTQ', explicitly modelled on 'classical' (pre-*Aspects* (Chomsky 1965) transformational grammar, which he argues to be closer in significant ways to Montague's system than the later 'standard' theory.

The same collection (Davis and Mithun 1979) – the proceedings of an interdisciplinary conference on Montague Grammar, Philosophy and Linguistics, held at the State University of New York at Albany in April 1977 – also includes James McCawley's (1979) careful comparison of the two types of grammar, 'Helpful hints to the ordinary working Montague Grammarian'. He compares the types and domains of rules used in the two and looks in detail at their analyses of raising and of English auxiliaries, suggesting areas where the Montagovian account could be improved by the incorporation of insights or devices from transformational grammar.

McCawley's intention is 'to demonstrate ... that various "abstract" syntactic analyses are not as irreconcilable with the "surfac-y" syntax of Montague grammar as might at first be thought' (1979: 104). Certainly the direct description of surface syntax looked like an important distinguishing feature of Montague Grammar as against the then dominant Standard Theory (although it is now prevalent among current linguistic theories). But another, perhaps even more fundamental distinction which is not made in any of these discussions is that of a categorial or Montague Grammar as a dependency grammar, in contrast to the phrase-structure base of a transformational grammar. Evidently, categorial grammars were still seen as phrase-structure grammars, albeit of an outstandingly precise and semantically well-informed variety.

But the informing objective remained a rigorous semantics, linked in a principled and systematic way to syntax. It was pursued further, into the area of word meaning, in David Dowty's (1979a) *Word Meaning and Montague Grammar: the Semantics of Verbs and Times in Generative Semantics and in Montague's PTQ*. This exploration of tense and verb classification considers a spectrum of semantic, syntactic and lexical aspects of its central issue. The principle of lexical decomposition is adopted from Generative Semantics, and given an explicit model-theoretic interpretation. Lexical rules are introduced into a Montague Grammar framework for the first time, initially for the formal description of derivational morphology in a form coherent with that of syntax, but with a crucial hint at their potential for direct description of 'syntax' itself, concluding that 'it now seems reasonable to me to suppose that virtually every instance of an observed governed transformation turns out to be analysable as a lexical rule in this theory' (1979a: 307). His ten illustrative examples include rules for inchoatives, causatives, reversative verbs and detransitivization (ibid.: 307–8). This, of course, has close parallels in Higgins (1976), Oehrle (1975) and such better-known contemporary milestones of the nascent lexicalist enterprise as Wasow's (1977) 'Transformations and the lexicon', Bresnan's (1978) 'A realistic transformational grammar', and Dowty's own (1978) 'Governed transformations as lexical rules in a Montague Grammar'. It can be seen as foreshadowing his (1982) lexical rules for category alternation, and the general current awareness of the inherent lexicalism of a categorial grammar.

As the semantic and syntactic traditions came together and their lexical basis became recognized, the third original informing discipline – mathematics, instantiated as computation – came to new life. Apparently separately from Dowty, but like him drawing on the work of Partee and others in Montague Grammar, Anthony Ades and Mark Steedman in 'On word-order' (1979) and 'On the order of words' (1982) proposed a model based on an incremental processor with a push-down stack, designed as a plausible model of the human sentence processor, using an 'extended categorial grammar' to describe syntax and semantics in parallel.

Complex categories are order-free in this system, with word order constrained by an adjacency condition on combination and by the directionality of the combination rules. Four of these are included, Forward Combination (application), Backward Combination, Forward Partial Combination (composition: see Ch.3.ii below), and Affix Cancellation; the first three are generalized by the 'dollar' convention, which represents the set of categories $\{X, X/Y$ for all $Y\}$ as $X\$$ (in other words, X and all functions into X: so, for example, $S\$$ stands for the set $\{S, S/N, (S/N)/N, S/S, ...\}$). The greater-than-context-free power which this induces in the case of composition (see Ch.4.ii.a below) was at least suspected at the time (Ades and Steedman 1982: 554, fn. 7).

At least as important as any details of the particular grammar used here is its explicit use of the concepts and insights of computation and psychology, of machine and human processing of language. The paper opens and closes with discussions of these issues, making it the first in which all the strands of the categorial tradition come together.

Steedman then focused on co-ordination (1983) and long-distance and crossing dependencies (1984), pointing out immediately the naturalness of a categorial syntax for right node raising (1983: 9), and extending the account to a range of English and Dutch co-ordinations and dependencies (1985a; for discussion see Ch.5.iii.d below). Dowty (1982) meanwhile suggested the derivation of grammatical relation assignments from the order in which arguments combine with a complex category.

A conference held in Tucson, Arizona, in June 1985 included, among others, papers by Lambek, Bach, Keenan, van Benthem and Oehrle. Michael Moortgat explored the use of disharmonic composition rules for discontinuous dependencies, Deirdre Wheeler spoke on phonology and Jack Hoeksema and Richard Janda on morphology, Carl Pollard presented Head-driven Phrase Structure Grammar (a half-categorial offshoot of GPSG), Mark Steedman proposed taking the 'combinators' used by Curry to define the foundations of the lambda-calculus directly as the basis of a categorial system, and David Dowty offered a categorial syntax for non-constituent co-ordination based on the extended use of type-raising and of functional composition (more on this below, Ch.5.iii.d). The proceedings of the conference (Oehrle *et al.* 1988) are probably the best readily available primary source for a wide range of recent categorial linguistics.

Since then, it seems, research within the categorial paradigm has spread rapidly. All the traditional strands and a number of newer ones are being developed, and there is a healthy growth in cross-linguistic work. Publications are multiplying, although unfortunately the majority are still technical reports or dissertations, and hard to get hold of. Categorial representation at both general conferences and specialist workshops is increasing. The highlights of work on specific topics in phonology, morphology and syntax are discussed in Chapter 5, and on more general issues in semantics, logic and algebra, language universals and psychological plausibility, word order and parsing in Chapter 6. The general position should, however, be clear from even this very partial view of the field. After decades as a minority interest, categorial grammars, in the quantity, quality and breadth of current research, are flourishing.

FURTHER READING

There are no published sources which expand on all or even a majority of the developments touched on in this chapter. The primary sources vary in their (intellectual) accessibility: Bar-Hillel and Steedman are particularly lucid and appealing, at one end of the scale, while at the other Montague is notoriously opaque, and best approached through Dowty *et al.* (1981) rather than directly. Buszkowski *et al.* (1988) reprint the classic papers by Lambek and Geach, and Marciszewski contributes a 'chronicle' of CG, but firmly from a logical, rather than linguistic, perspective. The Oehrle *et al.* collection (1988) is the best source for broader and more recent developments, and does give some historical insights, especially in the editors' Introduction and Emmon Bach's contribution.

3 Classical categorial grammar: the Lambek calculus

The minimal grammar outlined in the introduction, with the two atomic categories **S** and **N** and the two combination rules of forward and backward application, is the one used by Ajdukiewicz and Bar-Hillel (thus sometimes called an 'AB' grammar), and can handle a perhaps surprising range of natural language constructions. Almost all work in the field, however, from any perspective, has extended this basic system. The set of atomic categories is remarked by Ajdukiewicz and Bar-Hillel themselves to be inadequate, and is universally supplemented, at least by distinguishing (common) nouns (**CN** or **N**) from proper nouns or noun phrases (**PN** or **NP**). This will be explored below (Ch.4.i). The set of rules has also been extended, and it is a core of these extensions which I will consider here.

I have already discussed in general terms (Ch.2.iii.a above) the contribution made by Joachim Lambek's 1958 paper 'The mathematics of sentence structure', where he proposed an algebraic categorial calculus of 'syntactic types', or categories, for natural languages, which offered an algorithm for distinguishing sentences from non-sentences. This calculus is explicitly presented as a deductive system. Its axioms (in Lambek, result-on-top notation) are

$$x \to x$$

and

$$(xy)z \to x(yz), x(yz) \to (xy)z$$

with rules of inference

if $xy \to z$ then $x \to z/y$, if $xy \to z$ then $y \to x\backslash z$;
if $x \to z/y$ then $xy \to z$, if $y \to x\backslash z$ then $xy \to z$;
if $x \to y$ and $y \to z$ then $x \to z$.

On this basis, shown to be provable within this system, four rules are initially identified in the paper and motivated by examples of natural language analysis: (1) application, (2) associativity, (3) composition and (4) raising. These four constitute the 'free categorial grammar' of Cohen (1967). Also shown to be provable within the syntactic calculus are a rule of division, which is included in Moortgat's (1988b) discussion of the 'Lambek calculus', and a rule of 'flattening', omitted by Moortgat (probably because it depends on use of the product connective, which he also omits) but rediscovered in some recent work.

I shall give here some account of both the formal characteristics and natural language applicability of each of the five rules standardly taken to constitute the 'Lambek calculus', following Lambek's order of exposition. The rule schemata will be given in both the original notation (L), which makes many of them more transparent than in other forms, and in the Steedman notation (S) which I otherwise use consistently throughout. As I trace the use of each rule forward into later work, some examples will use notational conventions which have not yet been introduced, but these will be glossed where they are not transparent; note especially that many writers use much larger sets of apparent atomic categories, many of which are intended only as abbreviations for awkwardly complex categories.

It is important to bear in mind the distinction between binary rules, by which two categories can be combined, and unary rules, which convert one category into another. This is, of course, a restatement of the Saussurian distinction between the syntagmatic (combinatory, horizontal) and paradigmatic (alternatory, vertical) axes (for a fuller discussion of this distinction and of its application to a categorial calculus, see Wood 1987). There are clearly defined trade-offs between the complexity of the binary and unary rule systems – simple category assignments may require powerful combination rules, simple combination rules must sometimes be fed by strongly 'coerced' categories. Specific examples of such trade-offs will be mentioned as they arise in the course of this chapter; others will be found in the accounts of particular linguistic phenomena in Chapter 5.

3.i APPLICATION

The binary rule of function application, as already mentioned, is the first and simplest in any categorial calculus. A unidirectional system such as that of Ajdukiewicz has only one rule (a); a bidirectional system like Bar-Hillel's and Lambek's will have both forward (a) and backward (b) application (recall that the subscripts on the categories distinguish Lambek (L) from Steedman (S) notation – see Ch.1.iii above):

3.1 (a) $X/Y_LY \rightarrow X$
$X/Y_SY \rightarrow X$
(b) $Y\ Y\backslash X_L \rightarrow X$
$Y\ X\backslash Y_S \rightarrow X$

If the semantic value is spelled out (using italics following a colon), we have

3.2 (a) $X/Y{:}f_L\ Y{:}a \rightarrow X{:}f(a)$
(b) $Y{:}a\ Y\backslash X{:}f_L \rightarrow X{:}f(a)$

This is the only rule in the systems used by Ajdukiewicz and Bar-Hillel. Examples have been given in the discussion of their proposals above (Ch.2.iii.b,c) and in the introduction (Ch.1.ii). Lambek illustrates the rule with a number of simple sentences, including (numbering as in the original, pagination from Buszkowski *et al.* 1988):

3.3 (2) (poor John) works
n/n   n   n\s

(3) (John works) here
n   n\s   s\s

(4) John (never   works)
n   (n\s)/(n\s) n\s

(7) John   (likes Jane)
n   (n\s)/n   n

(Lambek 1958 [1988]: 155–6)

Bar-Hillel *et al.* (1960) proved the mutual formal equivalence of unidirectional and bidirectional CGs, the difference between them in practice for linguistic description (remarked by both themselves (1960: 101–2, quoted above, Ch.2.iii.b) and Chomsky (1963: 413, quoted above, Ch.2.ii)) being the possibility of 'natural' category assignments in a bidirectional CG. The proof followed as a corollary from the proof that these categorial grammars are strongly equivalent to type 2, context-free 'simple phrase-structure grammars'. As such, they are (as discussed above, Ch.2.iii.b) analogously inadequate for complete natural language description, notably when confronted with discontinuous dependencies.

3.ii ASSOCIATIVITY

Lambek's second rule is the unary rule which he calls associativity, which says that a function of two arguments, one on either side, can combine with them in either order: the bracketing can change without anything else being affected. This relation had been noted by Frege, Schönfinkel and Curry. Oehrle prefers to call it 'swapping', because associativity is standardly defined as a property of a single operator, but this is a relation between two operators. Confusion is certainly possible: I have retained the more commonly used terminology, but the reader has been warned.

3.4 $(X\backslash Y)/Z_L \leftrightarrow X\backslash(Y/Z)_L$
$(Y\backslash X)/Z_S \leftrightarrow (Y/Z)\backslash X_S$

With semantic values, in the far clearer original notation:

3.5 $(X\backslash Y)/Z{:}\lambda v_z \cdot \lambda v_x \cdot f(v_x)(v_z)_L \rightarrow X\backslash(Y/Z){:}\lambda v_x \cdot \lambda v_z \cdot f(v_x)(v_z)_L$
$X\backslash(Y/Z){:}\lambda v_x \cdot \lambda v_z \cdot f(v_x)(v_z)_L \rightarrow (X\backslash Y)/Z{:}\lambda v_z \cdot \lambda v_x \cdot f(v_x)(v_z)_L$

Note the first use of lambda- (λ-) abstraction to 'bind' the value of variables within a formula. If v is a variable of type A (say), then $\lambda v.f$ (the binding of v within the scope of the function f) denotes a function with domain A whose value, for any object a of type A, is the value of f which results from anchoring every free occurrence of v in f to the value a. Here the semantic value of $(\mathbf{x}\backslash\mathbf{y})/\mathbf{z}$ is a function which first finds the semantic value of the variable v_z, corresponding to $\mathbf{z}$, the first argument to be incorporated in the syntactic derivation. It then finds v_x, the semantics of $\mathbf{x}$ in the syntax. The function f takes v_x as its first argument, v_z as its second, their values now appropriately bound. The change in syntactic bracketing means that the semantic function for $\mathbf{x}\backslash(\mathbf{y}/\mathbf{z})$ binds v_x before v_z, but the order of arguments to f remains constant.

The principal example given by Lambek of the use of associativity (he suggests also the categories of *never*, *for* and *and*; 1958 [1988]: 156) is that of a transitive verb which can combine syntactically with either its object or subject first. In the semantic interpretation, the verb is the functor, the order of its arguments indicating which

nominal is subject and which is object. Associativity guarantees that
the nominals will be assigned to the correct roles in the semantics
regardless of the order in which they are incorporated in the syntax.
In addition to the derivation

3.6 (7) John (likes   Jane)
     n   (n\s)/n n

given above (3.3), there is a symmetrical derivation, with identical
interpretation,

3.7 (7′) (John   likes) Jane
     n   n\(s/n) n

(Lambek 1958 [1988]: 156)

Indeed, Lambek suggests that, rather than using brackets to distinguish between effectively equivalent types, one can use an unbracketed, neutral form such as **n\s/n** to generalize over both.

The effect of associativity on the descriptive power of the grammar
is that it offers alternative bracketings, and thus, implicitly, alternative 'constituent' structures for a sentence, with equivalent semantic
interpretations (unless the relative scopes of quantifiers are altered) –
the property now known as 'spurious ambiguity'. Something like this
had been intimated by Bar-Hillel (1953: 70; Ch.2.iii.b above);
Lambek gives it a fully formal basis. In most cases it will not affect
the grammaticality judgements for particular sentences, the recog-
nizing power of the grammar: it causes a procedural, processing problem (to which we will return later, Ch.6.v), but is irrelevant in
declarative terms. The exceptions are constructions which violate conventional constituent structure, such as 'non-constituent co-
ordination'. This will be discussed more fully below (Ch.5.iii.d);
briefly, as soon as we have a way of describing *John likes* as a connex
substring, a 'derivational constituent', of category **s/n**, we can conjoin two such substrings and accept *John likes, and Mary adores*, ...
as a well-formed sentence.

3.iii COMPOSITION

The second (and last) binary rule to be introduced is that of function
composition, again both forward (a) and backward (b; notice that this
rule is, again, more perspicuous in Lambek's notation, where an argument element has the same position within a functor category as the

argument itself relative to the functor in the surface string). Where application must take a complete argument – either really atomic, or prepared to behave as if atomic for purposes of combination, within brackets – function composition, as its name should suggest, allows a function needing a given argument to 'compose' with another function which outputs that argument as its value, with a result whose value is that of the 'functor' function and whose argument is that of the 'argument' function:

3.8 (a) $X/Y_LY/Z_L \rightarrow X/Z_L$
$X/Y_SY/Z_S \rightarrow X/Z_S$
(b) $Z\backslash Y_LY\backslash X_L \rightarrow Z\backslash X_L$
$Y\backslash Z_SX\backslash Y_S \rightarrow X\backslash Z_S$

Complete with semantic values:

3.9 (a) $X/Y{:}f_L\ Y/Z{:}g_L \rightarrow X/Z{:}\lambda v_z \cdot f(g(v_z))_L$
(b) $Z\backslash Y{:}g_L Y\backslash X{:}f_L \rightarrow X\backslash Z{:}\lambda v_z \cdot f(g(v_z))_L$

That is, given a function from **X** to **Y** with semantics f and a function from **Y** to **Z** with semantics g, we can 'compose' them to give a single function directly from **X** to **Z**, whose semantic formula binds the value of the variable v_z such that f holds of $(g$ of $v_z)$ – in other words, both functions have applied to the last argument they find – regardless of surface word order. This gives the system used in Karlgren (1978) and Ades and Steedman (1982).

Lambek introduces composition for the combination of a subject pronoun, of category **s/(n\s)**, or object pronoun, of category **(s/n)\s**, with a transitive verb of the unbracketed category **n\s/n** discussed above: the sentence *he likes him*, with the category assignments **s/(n\s) n\s/n (s/n)\s**, can thus be derived either by forward-composing *he likes* to **s/n** or backward-composing *likes him* to **n\s**, with the second, final step in the derivation taken by application (backward in the first instance, forward in the second):

3.10   he   likes   him
       s/(n\s) n\s/n   (s/n)\s
      —————————>C
         s/n
        —————————————<A
             s

3.11   he   likes   him
    s/(n\s) n\s/n (s/n)\s
             ————————<C
            n\s
     ————————————>A
       s

                              (1958 [1988]: 162–3)

The motivation for including composition in the grammar of Ades and Steedman (1982) is somewhat different, arising from their procedural, computational (and psychological) objective of immediate left-to-right interpretation. A sentence with a complex auxiliary-verb cluster, like *John must have been eating beans*, has a conventional entirely right-branching phrase-structure analysis which can be mirrored precisely using application, but could not begin to be interpreted until the end of the string was reached, as the successive operations of (forward) application would have to work their way, as it were, from back to front of the string. By the use of composition (or 'Partial Combination', as it is called there) a partial interpretation can be built up immediately for such fragments as *must have* (1982: 526–7). The principle can be illustrated with a simpler example, the derivation of a noun phrase with multiple adjectives. Application can only work through from right to left (3.12), composition from left to right (3.13), although the resulting semantic interpretation is the same in either case, so the 'ambiguity' is again 'spurious':

3.12   that small hungry brown dog
    N/N N/N N/N   N/N   N
                   ————————>A
                 N
             ————————————>A
           N
       ————————————————>A
      N
  ————————————————>A
    N

3.13 that small hungry brown dog
    N/N N/N N/N N/N   N
    ────────>C
      N/N
      ────────────>C
        N/N
        ────────────────>C
          N/N
          ────────────────────>A
            N

Forward composition is used extensively in Steedman's and much other subsequent work; backward composition is used in Dowty's (1988) account of non-constituent co-ordination, in such derivations as:

3.14 John saw Mary yesterday and   Bill   today
    e   tv vp\tv vp\vp Conj vp\tv vp\vp
               ──────────<C   ──────────<C
             vp\tv   vp\tv
             ─────────────────────────────────
                        vp\tv
             ────────────────────────<A
                 vp
        ────────────────>A
          t

                             (1988: 170)

3.15 John gave Mary a book and Susan a record
    e   ttv tv\ttv vp\tv Conj tv\ttv vp\tv
               ──────────<C   ──────────<C
             vp\ttv   vp\ttv
             ──────────────────────────────
                      vp\ttv
             ────────────────────────<A
               vp
        ──────────────>A
         t

                             (ibid.: 172)

(Note the use of value-first notation, and the abbreviated complex categories; the principles on which those categories are assigned will be discussed in the next section. **'Conj'** is a functor which combines two identical categories to form one of that same category – for more detailed discussion see Ch.5.iii.d.)

This simple form of composition does not by itself extend the weak generative power of the grammar (although, as we will see (Ch.4.ii.a), its generalized, recursive form does). However, by making possible a number of different, semantically equivalent derivations for a given string – the property of 'spurious ambiguity' noted above – it plays a significant part in some classic combinations which do, and in many of the trade-offs alluded to above. Some proposals eliminate composition in favour of an 'application-only' system with additional unary rules, such as associativity, which massage categories into the correct form to 'feed' application. Bouma (1989) re-introduces Lambek's 'product' connective (see Ch.4.ii below) in order to do without composition and thus to eliminate spurious ambiguity, Uszkoreit (1986) suggests assigning complex categories in the lexicon in such a way as to eliminate a rule of composition as an option for the same reason, and Zeevat (1988) argues for unification-based devices instead of the composition rule. Others, on the other hand, welcome the economy it allows in the unary rule system.

3.iv RAISING

In Lambek's example of functional composition, the pronoun *he* was taken to be lexically assigned the category $s/(n\backslash s)$ – a function which will return a sentence, given a following predicate – to indicate its restriction to occurrence in subject position. The object pronoun *him* was analogously lexically specified as $(s/n)\backslash s$, a function to a sentence from a preceding sentence-given-a-following-noun. The unary rule of type-raising allows an unmarked noun to take on either of these specified categories, subject (a) or object (b), or indeed any atomic category **X** to become a functor looking for a functor looking for **X**:

3.16 (a) $X \rightarrow Y/(X\backslash Y)_L$
$\qquad X \rightarrow Y/(Y\backslash X)_S$
(b) $X \rightarrow (Y/X)\backslash Y_L$
$\qquad X \rightarrow Y\backslash(Y/X)_S$

with the semantic interpretation imposing a λ-binding on the function:

3.17 (a) $X{:}a \rightarrow Y/(X\backslash Y){:}\lambda v \cdot v(a)_L$
(b) $X{:}a \rightarrow (Y/X)\backslash Y{:}\lambda v \cdot v(a)_L$

The other linguistic example Lambek gives is that of a prepositional phrase in which the preposition requires an object-type argument and the nominal argument must be raised to match it.

Raising, especially of subjects, is a familiar rule in the semantic tradition. It underlies Montague's (1973) assignment to 'term-phrases' of the category **t/IV**, and is used in the analysis of quantifier phrases by Lewis (1972). Although often innocent, it need not preserve logical implications: Partee and Rooth (1983) point out three cases in English where intended readings could not (easily) be derived without raising. These involve conjoined intensional (*John wants and needs two secretaries*) or extensional (*John caught and ate a fish*) verbs (1983: 365–6), wide-scope *or* (*The department is looking for a phonologist or a phonetician* (*but I don't know which*) (ibid.: 374) – see further Rooth and Partee 1982), and common-noun conjunction (*Most men and women swim* cannot be paraphrased as *Most hermaphrodites swim* (ibid.: 374)).

In syntactic description, although raising could in principle create all sorts of silly new raised functor categories, they will not lead to the recognition of silly new sentence structures, because there will be no source of corresponding silly new arguments for the functors. Raising a sentence-initial **NP** to **S/(S\NP)**, as below, makes possible a new derivation pattern for the already derivable string **NP S\NP**. But raising, say, **Adj** to **VP/(VP\Adj)** (using abbreviated categories for clarity) will not suddenly license strings like *****Adj V**, as there is no source for the argument **VP\Adj** (a function to a verb phrase from a preceding adjective) in English. The one area where raising does extend the weak generative power of the grammar is in the description of non-standard 'constituent' structures, as in 3.19 below (see further Ch.5.iii.c, 5.iii.d).

Steedman (1985a) assigns the raised nominal category **S/FVP** (**FVP** = 'finite verb phrase', an abbreviation for **S\NP**) to subjects, citing Montague and other work in semantics as a precedent. This is shown to permit entirely left-branching sentence structures (ibid.: 538), thus taking to its conclusion the move towards incremental derivation which motivated his introduction of function composition – for example (notation adapted slightly):

3.18 <u>I can</u> believe that she   will   eat   <u>those cakes</u>
    S/VP VP/S′ S′/S S/FVP FVP/VP VP/NP   NP
    ————————>C
      S/S′
    ————————————>C
       S/S
       ————————————>C
         S/FVP
         ————————————————>C
           S/VP
           ————————————————————>C
              S/NP
              ————————————————————————>A
                    S

This incidentally makes possible the now standard treatment of right node raised constructions (ibid.: 541 – for more detailed discussion see Ch.5.iii.d):

3.19
Harry   cooked   and   Mary   ate   the beans that I bought from Alice
S/FVP FVP/NP Conj S/FVP FVP/NP   NP
————————>C   ————————>C
  S/NP   S/NP
        S/NP
        ————————————————————————>A
          S

This account using composition and raising should be compared to the left-associative bracketing, and account of right node raising, available in a grammar using application and associativity (see Ch.3.ii above). The two different derivations give the same semantic interpretation for a given sentence, as Moortgat (1988b: 21–2) demonstrates, and are thus another good example of spurious ambiguity. Notice too the way in which composition and raising complement each other, the unary rule providing the category necessary for the binary rule to be applicable. This derivation for right node raising is characteristic in being possible only with both.

Dowty (1988) adopts in his discussion of non-constituent co-ordination both subject-raising, with the resulting analysis of right node raising, and wider applications of a generalized raising rule to a range of object positions, in three 'stages', motivated both semantically and syntactically. A direct object, initially the following argument of a transitive verb (**tv**, an abbreviation for (**S\NP**)/**NP**) to form a verb phrase, is raised to become a function over a preceding transitive verb to form a verb phrase, thus **vp\tv**. An indirect object is a function from a preceding ditransitive verb (**ttv**) to (effectively) a transitive verb, thus **tv\ttv** – note in the examples below that the non-standard 'constituent' *gave Mary* shows the same behaviour as the single word *saw*; both need a following direct object to form a verb phrase.

3.20, cf. 3.14 John saw Mary yesterday and   Bill   today
            e   tv vp\tv vp\vp Conj vp\tv vp\vp

3.21, cf. 3.15 John gave Mary a book and Susan a record
            e   ttv tv\ttv vp\tv Conj tv\ttv vp\tv

These various raised object types can be composed (extending the proposals of Steedman (1985a) for the description of Dutch verb-raising constructions) to produce as 'derivational constituents' a range of non-canonical conjuncts (as shown more fully above, Ch.3.iii; more on this below, Ch.5.iii.d).

In the light of the general recent move towards declarative, mono-tonic grammar formalisms (see Shieber 1986), these proposals point up an important issue about the status of all unary rules: how exactly are they to be interpreted, and how can they be used? One could take the rule of raising to be a declarative well-formedness condition, in the spirit of GPSG meta-rules or indeed any lexicalist linguistic descrip-tion: if a certain item has the category X then it can also have the category $Y/(Y\backslash X)$, presumably by lexical assignment. Or the rule could have a procedural interpretation, as might seem natural in a computational implementation: given category X, apply the rule to that category to produce the category $Y/(Y\backslash X)$. There is a tendency to favour the declarative interpretation (although the issue is not always openly faced).

A related issue has to do with the formal and computational proper-ties of raising. This is the first rule in the calculus to be recursive – an argument can be raised over its functor, the original functor raised again over the new category of the original argument, and so on *ad infinitum*. It thus opens an infinite space, and, implemented procedurally, a fatal infinite regression. The recursion can be bounded in a number of ways, usually by limiting raised categories to those given in the lexicon, or applying the rule only 'on demand', when it

offers the only possible way to form a derivation or correct interpretation for a sentence. These are effective enough as solutions to the practical problems, but compromise the 'free algebra' of the system; a
compromise which worries some categorialists more than others.

3.v DIVISION

The final rule in the Lambek calculus is a unary rule of division,
applied to both sides of the main slash operator in a functor category:

3.22 (a) $X/Y_L \rightarrow (X/Z)/(Y/Z)_L$
            $X/Y_S \rightarrow (X/Z)/(Y/Z)_S$
      (b) $X\backslash Y_L \rightarrow (Z\backslash X)\backslash(Z\backslash Y)_L$
            $Y\backslash X_S \rightarrow (Y\backslash Z)\backslash(X\backslash Z)_S$

The semantic interpretation binds two variables nested in the scope of
the functor:

3.23 (a) $X/Y{:}f_L \rightarrow (X/Z)/(Y/Z){:}\lambda v_z \cdot \lambda v_y \cdot f(v_z(v_y))_L$
      (b) $X\backslash Y{:}f_L \rightarrow (Z\backslash X)\backslash(Z\backslash Y){:}\lambda v_z \cdot \lambda v_y \cdot f(v_z(v_y))_L$

This could be paraphrased (for both directions) as saying that a
functor which forms **X** with a **Y** can become a functor which forms
X-given-a-**Z** if it finds **Y**-given-a-**Z**. Notice the similarity of this unary
rule in its effect to the binary rule of function composition: each
allows a function to find, as it were, only part of its argument, carrying forward the remainder (more on this shortly). As with raising,
division might be used to produce fantastical functor categories, but
without appropriate arguments these will be harmless.

   Lambek himself includes this rule almost in passing, among a
number of other rules 'provable' in a system based on application,
associativity and composition. He uses it to capture the generalization
that 'every sentence-modifying adverb is also a predicate-modifying
adverb, symbolically, $s\backslash s \rightarrow (n\backslash s)\backslash(n\backslash s)$' (1958 [1988]: 165) and thus to
allow alternative analyses of *John works here* as either (3.24) or (3.25):

3.24 (3)   (John works) here
                 n   n\s   s\s

3.25 John (works   here)
          n   n\s   (n\s)\(n\s)

He sketches a proof of the validity of division whereby $z/y \rightarrow$ $(z/x)/(y/x)$ follows from the composition rule $(z/y)(y/x) \rightarrow z/x$ by the axiom $xy \rightarrow z \Rightarrow x \rightarrow z/y$ (if the sequence xy reduces to z, then x must be a function from y to z) (ibid.: 164).

Moortgat (1987b; 1988b: 23), following Zielonka (1981), adds to these rules of division of a main functor similarly symmetrical rules of 'inverse' division of a subordinate functor, which have the effect of 'rais[ing] the type of the subordinate functor until it can consume the main functor by simple application' (ibid.: 15):

3.26 (a) $X/Y_L \rightarrow (Z/X)\backslash(Z/Y)_L$
$X/Y_S \rightarrow (Z/Y)\backslash(Z/X)_S$
(b) $Y\backslash X_L \rightarrow (Y\backslash Z)/(X\backslash Z)_L$
$X\backslash Y_S \rightarrow (Z\backslash Y)/(Z\backslash X)_S$

differing critically from the first form of the rule in the relative scopes of the functor and the first variable:

3.27 (a) $X/Y{:}f_L \rightarrow (Z/X)\backslash(Z/Y){:}\lambda v_z \cdot \lambda v_y \cdot v_z(f(v_y))_L$
(b) $Y\backslash X{:}f_L \rightarrow (Y\backslash Z)/(X\backslash Z){:}\lambda v_z \cdot \lambda v_y \cdot v_z(f(v_y))_L$

He illustrates the linguistic use of the two division rules with alternative derivations of the adjective phrase *related to Mary* (categories in Lambek notation, notation for derivation paths slightly adapted):

3.28   related   to   Mary
 AP/PP PP/NP   NP
 ————————————*
 (AP/NP)/(PP/NP)
 ————————————————>A
 AP/NP
 ————————————————————>A
 AP

*division of main functor

3.29 related   to   Mary
 AP/PP PP/NP NP
 ——————————————**
 (AP/PP)\(AP/NP)
 —————————————————<A
 AP/NP
 —————————————————————>A
 AP

**division of subordinate functor

 (1988b: 24)

Notice that both derivations move from left to right, and use application as their only binary rule. With application only, a nonincremental derivation is still possible:

```
3.30 related    to    Mary
     AP/PP PP/NP  NP
          ―――――――>A
             PP
     ―――――――――――>A
          AP
```

In this case, in a CG with first-order function composition, division (which, being recursive, makes all orders of composition provable) would be unnecessary, even for an incremental derivation:

```
3.31 related    to    Mary
     AP/PP PP/NP  NP
     ―――――――――>C
        AP/NP
     ――――――――――>A
          A
```

Division preserves word order and (unlike raising) logical implications, but, being recursive, extends the power of the system to 'structural completeness', where, for any grammatical string, any substring can be formed as a 'constituent' and any item in the substring can be its head. Raising is recursive, but affects only which of a pair of adjacent categories is functor and which argument. With division, on the other hand, to quote Moortgat:

> If a sequence of categories X1, ..., Xn reduces to Y, there is a reduction to Y for any bracketing of X1, ..., Xn into constituents. Among these representations, there is no privileged one as far as the categorial calculus is concerned.
>
> (1987a: 5)

This is why he takes it to be 'the characteristic theorem of [the] L[ambek calculus], i.e. the theorem which distinguishes this system from weaker categorial calculi' (Moortgat 1987a: 4). Structural completeness, of course, induces the extreme of spurious ambiguity, the maximum number of possible derivation paths converging on the same semantic interpretation.

A slightly different form of division rule was suggested independently by Geach (1972), and indeed is commonly referred to as the 'Geach rule'. It is proposed there as an extension to the Ajdukiewicz system, which included only application, not composition: Geach explicitly presents it as a recursive converse to the Ajdukiewicz 'multiplying-out' rule, initially to capture the difference in negative scope of the Aristotelian examples *ou petetai Socrates* ('Socrates is not flying') and *ou pas anthropos petetai* ('not every man is flying'). The rule (recast in Steedman notation, and directionally neutral) takes the form

$$\text{If } \mathbf{a} \ \mathbf{b} \to \mathbf{c}, \ \mathbf{a} \ \mathbf{b}|\mathbf{d} \to \mathbf{c}|\mathbf{d}$$

and thus

$$\text{Since } \mathbf{s}|\mathbf{s} \ \mathbf{s} \to \mathbf{s}, \ \mathbf{s}|\mathbf{s} \ \mathbf{s}|\mathbf{x} \to \mathbf{s}|\mathbf{x}.$$

And this covers all cases in which negation, of category $\mathbf{s}|\mathbf{s}$, operates upon a sentence of structure $\mathbf{s}|\mathbf{x} \ \mathbf{x}$. The string of expressions categorized as $\mathbf{s}|\mathbf{s} \ \mathbf{s}|\mathbf{x} \ \mathbf{x}$ may be split up in two ways into S[yntactically] C[onnex] sub-strings; namely, we may regard negation ($\mathbf{s}|\mathbf{s}$) as operating on the whole sentence categorized as $\mathbf{s}|\mathbf{x} \ \mathbf{x}$; or, we may regard it as combining with the $\mathbf{s}|\mathbf{x}$ expression to form a complex $\mathbf{s}|\mathbf{x}$ expression, which then combines with the $\mathbf{x}$ expression to form a sentence.

(1972: 485)

The same rule offers a ready-made account of non-constituent co-ordination (see further Ch.5.iii.d).

This rule, in which one item on each side of a reduction schema rather than of a complex category is divided, has the effect of offering a proof of the validity of composition – in fact, since division is recursive, a proof for recursive, that is, generalized, composition (see Ch.4.ii.a; I again translate the notation):

$$\mathbf{s}|\mathbf{s} \ \mathbf{s} \to \mathbf{s}$$
$$\text{ergo, } \mathbf{s}|\mathbf{s} \ \mathbf{s}|(\mathbf{s}|\mathbf{n}) \to \mathbf{s}|(\mathbf{s}|\mathbf{n})$$

$$\text{Since } \mathbf{s}|(\mathbf{s}|\mathbf{n}) \ \mathbf{s}|\mathbf{n} \to \mathbf{s}, \ \mathbf{s}|(\mathbf{s}|\mathbf{n}) \ (\mathbf{s}|\mathbf{n})|\mathbf{n} \to \mathbf{s}|\mathbf{n}$$

(ibid.: 486–7)

This should be contrasted with Lambek's account, in which it is composition which is given and division derived from it: what is constant is that the two are completely interdependent. Indeed, as the adjective phrase examples above show, this is one of the classic trade-offs in the design of a CG: the question of whether recursive power should come from the unary rule set (through division) or the binary rules (through composition).

FURTHER READING

Lambek's original (1958) paper is at last generally available, in Buszkowski *et al.* (1988), and is a clear, exciting programmatic statement well worth looking at (sections 8 and 9, on the Gentzen sequent calculus, are both the least accessible and the least important for linguists). Geach (1972) is also reprinted in the same volume: again, his breadth of vision and strong sense of possibility are well worth the struggle with Polish notation. Of current work, Moortgat (1988b) is an excellent introduction and discussion, distinctive in its respect both for Lambek's algebra and for linguistics, to which I am indebted for many important points in this chapter.

Lambda calculus forms the basis for most formal semantic systems for categorial grammars: for a gentle introduction to the basics, see Cresswell (1988: 121–3); for a more thorough introduction Dowty *et al.* (1981), Stoy (1977) or Hindley and Seldin (1986).

4 Generalized categorial grammars

Trying to keep everything strictly CF or pure-categorial has
something of the dubious pleasure of dryfly fishing. You may
eventually catch a trout but sometimes wet flies or worms work
better.

(Bach 1984: 9)

The particular categorial calculus described by Lambek is a convenient 'benchmark' among CGs, clearly stated, carefully studied and
thus from many perspectives well understood. It should be clear by
now, however, that the Lambek calculus is only one point (albeit not
an arbitrary one) on a long scale of complexity, ranging from the
minimal 'AB' (Ajdukiewicz/Bar-Hillel) grammar described in the
introduction (two atomic categories, **S** and **N**, and one, binary, rule
of function application), through the Lambek calculus ('L'), to many
other systems which extend their formal and/or linguistic power in
many different ways. Most extend the set of atomic categories, at least
to some extent; a few extend the set of connectives; the focus of debate
is on extensions to the set of rules – what rules can be added, what
formal and what descriptive power they add to a grammar, how excessive power might be constrained, which is the best trade-off between
binary and unary rules, or between generality and restriction, or
between formal purity and linguistic accuracy and so on.

This chapter surveys some of the more significant of the various
proposed extensions to L – atomic categories, connectives, rules of all
sorts and finally the superficially very different incarnation of the
essential categorial enterprise in Unification Categorial Grammars.

4.i EXTENDING THE SET OF 'ATOMIC' CATEGORIES

The original, semantically motivated minimal set of atomic categories was restricted to two, **t** and **e** – in their more linguistically oriented form, **S** and **N**. For any sort of serious linguistic description, this is not sufficiently expressive. The observant reader will have noticed the high proportion of proper names in the example sentences used so far, and may be feeling uneasy. Even Montague distinguished 'terms' from 'entities', and Ajdukiewicz (1935: 209–10) discusses the apparent need for distinct categories for 'singular' and 'general' names in 'ordinary' language. Bar-Hillel takes **S** to be sentence and **N** to be 'the other basic categories' – that is how the complementizer 'that' comes to be represented as **n**/[s] – but (to be fair) adds that 'the categories dealt with so far are too gross to be applicable to ordinary languages' (1953: 63), pointing in particular to the need for a finer subdivision of **N**.

It is, in fact, clearly necessary on both semantic and syntactic grounds, and almost universal in current categorial practice, to allow both **N** (noun) and **NP** (noun phrase) as distinct atomic categories, thus extending the set to three. (Some systems use **CN** (common noun) and **PN** (proper noun) for this distinction.) It now becomes possible to distinguish determiners from adjectives: an adjective is a function from a noun to a noun (**N/N**), while a determiner takes a noun to a noun phrase (**NP/N**). The derivation given earlier to illustrate the use of function composition (3.13) now becomes

4.1   that small hungry brown dog
     NP/N N/N N/N   N/N   N
     ————————>C
      NP/N
      ————————————>C
        NP/N
        ————————————————>C
          NP/N
          ————————————————>A
            NP

This predicts accurately that any number of adjectives can precede a noun, but only one determiner. And, since the category of a transitive verb is not (**S\N**)/**N** but (**S\NP**)/**NP**, it also predicts that *I see a dog* is grammatical but **I see small dog* is not:

```
4.2   I      see      a      dog
     NP  (S\NP)/NP  NP/N   N
                    ─────────>A
                        NP
            ──────────────────>A
                  S\NP
     ──────────────────<A
              S
```

```
4.3   I        see   small dog
     NP   (S\NP)/NP  N/N   N
                    ─────────>A
                      N
     ──────────────────>A
              fail
```

The set of atomic categories **S**, **NP**, **N** is thus clearly defensible and descriptively valuable, and so is widely adopted and uncontentious. The only other potentially atomic category which is commonly accepted (by those who work on the phenomena which require it) is a distinct category for embedded sentences, **S′**. It has mainly been introduced for syntactic reasons, such as the accurate description of verbs which require an embedded sentence as complement, and of complementizers, which (in English) take a normal sentence and turn it into an embedded one:

```
4.4  Chris    said    that   Tigger caught a dove
      NP   (S\NP)/S′  S′/S          S
                             ──────────────>A
                        S′
            ──────────────────────>A
                  S\NP
     ──────────────────────────<A
              S
```

In other languages, the syntactic need to distinguish between main and embedded sentences can be even greater, as it affects, for example, the position of the verb in German and Dutch clauses, and the tense of the verb in French. Some semantic motivation can be found, too, in, for example, the semantics of belief, and the characteristics of 'opaque' contexts.

Other seemingly atomic categories can be found in the literature, many, but not all of them intended simply as abbreviations for their cumbersomely long full functorial equivalents. A good example is the use of **REL** in Pareschi (1988: 272, following Steedman and Moortgat) to describe the relative pronoun *which* as **REL/(S/NP)**, leading to derivations like

4.5   which   I   ate

     REL/(S/NP)   S/(S\NP)   (S\NP)/NP

                      ————————————>C

                             S/NP

    ————————————————>A

                 REL

Pareschi notes explicitly in a footnote that

> For simplicity's sake, we treat here relative clauses as constituents of atomic type. But in reality relative clauses are noun modifiers, that is, functions from nouns to nouns. Therefore, the … atomic type … should be thought of as shorthand for the corresponding complex type.
>
>   (ibid.)

Similarly, **PP** can often be found as an abbreviation, especially when it is preferred to maintain the ambiguity (or generalization, if you prefer) of that traditional category, which famously can be a back-modifier of either nouns or verb phrases, thus either **N\N** or **(S\NP)\(S\NP)**:

4.6   see   the boy   with   a telescope

   (S\NP)/NP   NP   ((S\NP)\(S\NP))/NP   NP

   ——————>A ——————————————>A

       S\NP   (S\NP)\(S\NP)

   ————————————————————————<A

               S\NP

```
4.7    see      the boy     with     a bicycle
     (S\NP)/NP NP/N  N    (N\N)/NP    NP
                               ─────────────────>A
                                    N\N
                          ─────────────────────<A
                 N
              ───────>A
                NP
     ──────────────────────>A
            S\NP
```

There are cases where the status of **PP** is less clear: for example, it is sometimes used to distinguish the two objects of a ditransitive verb:

```
4.8 Chris       gave        a fish  to Tigger
     NP    ((S\NP)/PP)/NP    NP        PP
           ──────────────────────>A
                 (S\NP)/PP
           ─────────────────────────────>A
                      S\NP
     ───────────────────────────────<A
                  S
```

This is more standard, and simpler, than Dowty's analysis of ditransitive constructions, which raises the two objects to different raised categories (see 3.15 above), but it does somewhat fudge the issue of the status of **PP**. Moortgat (1988b: 11) explicitly takes **PP** and **AP** to be atomic predicates when they serve as complements, as in the ditransitive case, but complex when they serve as modifiers. Another approach is to introduce feature-marking on **NP**s, possibly for case, so distinguishing accusative, direct object **NP**$_{acc}$ from benefactive, indirect object **NP**$_{ben}$. If one is worried about smuggling in unintended and possibly contentious semantic implications, the direct object could be **NP** and the indirect object **NP**$_{to}$. Either way, the two objects of a ditransitive verb are distinguished while avoiding the use of **PP** as a complement category with any status: this attractive solution is central to the expressive power of unification-based CGs, which will be discussed below (Ch.4.v).

There are, of course, similar problems with verbs and verb phrases, for which similar extensions to the set of atomic categories have occasionally been proposed. Lambek, as well as acknowledging the inadequacy of **N**, remarks that 'A more thorough analysis of the English

verb phrase would compel us to introduce further primitive types for
the infinitive and the two kinds of participles of intransitive verbs'
(1958 [1988]: 158). Ades and Steedman (1982), as we have seen (3.18),
use **FVP**, 'finite verb phrase' – equivalent to (non-directional) $S|NP$
– distinguished from **VP**, to describe the internal structure of complex auxiliary-verb clusters; they also use C_{en} and C_{ing} for the two
participles, as well as C_{that} in the description of sentence-embedding,
but do not discuss the issue of what should constitute the set of atomic
categories.

There are other, finer-grained distinctions which need to be made
in order to deal with inflexional morphology and agreement. We have
touched on the case-marking of NPs, and number, gender, person,
tense and possibly other factors must also be accommodated in a
categorial notation for adequate linguistic description. This has occasionally been recognized in a somewhat *ad hoc* and piecemeal fashion
– for example, Lambek distinguishes plural from singular forms by
starring them, in category assignments like

4.9   John   likes   girls
      n   n\s/n*   n*

4.10 Men   like   Jane
      n*   n*\s/n   n

while admitting that this 'introduces an undesirable multiplicity of
types' (1958 [1988]: 158). To balance expressiveness with economy
and generalization, one would like to encode such characteristics as
features on categories, rather than as constituting distinct categories
by themselves. This is exactly the approach taken to its logical conclusion in unification-based CGs, where all information is encoded as
feature values – this will be discussed more fully below (Ch.4.v).

The other most significant enrichment of the category system has
been the systematic development of 'polymorphic' (many-shaped)
categories. One type of polymorphism has been current since Lambek,
the change in the form of a particular category through the application of a unary rule, such as raising or division. As used more recently,
however (especially in the context of unification), the term generally
refers to the use of variables, not just in abstract rule schemata where
we have seen them so far, but in the actual categories themselves. The
classic example is the category assigned to conjunctions (conveniently
ignored in 3.14 and 3.15 above). A conjunction can apply to two
nouns to form a noun, two noun phrases to form a noun phrase, two

verbs to form a verb, two sentences to form a sentence and so on. To avoid assigning to *and*, *or*, *but* in the lexicon an indefinite number of distinct categories, among which they would appear to be ambiguous on every occasion, and to capture the essential generalization that a conjunction takes two of anything to one of the same, the category of a conjunction is generally given as (some variant of) **X\X/X**, that is, exactly, a functor which takes two **X**s, one from each side, and forms an **X** as result. Wood (1987) maps the broad space of paradigmatic rules – that is, unary rules, or polymorphic alternations – in CGs; Moortgat (1988b: Ch. 5) discusses some formal aspects of polymorphism and appropriate proof procedures, in a fairly technical way.

4.ii EXTENDING THE SET OF CONNECTIVES

Few of these extensions to the category system extend the generative power of a CG, although they clearly have serious effects on descriptive power and expressiveness. There have also been proposals to extend the set of connectives, some of which are equally innocent, some less so.

The directionally neutral 'slash' connective | forming complex, functor categories was the first, and for a long time the only connective in a CG; it is still widely used in semantic analyses, where surface word order is not at issue. More serious consideration of syntax led Bar-Hillel to introduce the two directional slashes, forward / and backward \, and these have been almost universally used in syntactic description since then. Some grammars include all three, using the neutral slash as a generalization where variations in word order are possible, as in the position of some English sentence modifiers:

4.11 <u>Michael played football</u> yesterday

$$\frac{\overset{\text{S}}{} \qquad \overset{\text{S|S}}{}}{\text{S}} < A$$

4.12 Yesterday <u>Michael played football</u>

$$\frac{\overset{\text{S|S}}{} \qquad \overset{\text{S}}{}}{\text{S}} > A$$

The Lambek calculus includes the two directional slashes, forming rightward- and leftward-looking functors, and a third connective, the 'product' $*$, which forms an ordered pair – not a functor – from two adjacent categories. A product in a directional categorial calculus is an ordered pair of categories which functions as a single (complex) category: it can serve as the argument of a functor category, as a conjunct in co-ordinate constructions and so on. The ordering is crucial, although in other systems 'products', strictly so called, may be unordered. Lambek does not use the product connective for any of his linguistic examples, but it is used (implicitly in the original notation; I include it here for clarity, and give functor categories result-first) in the basic rules of inference

$$\text{if } \mathbf{x}*\mathbf{y} \rightarrow \mathbf{z} \text{ then } \mathbf{x} \rightarrow \mathbf{z}/\mathbf{y}; \text{ if } \mathbf{x}*\mathbf{y} \rightarrow \mathbf{z} \text{ then } \mathbf{y} \rightarrow \mathbf{z}\backslash\mathbf{x}$$

which are needed to prove the validity of raising and division (Lambek 1958 [1988]: 164). He also shows to be provable the rules (again in the present notation)

$$\mathbf{x} \rightarrow (\mathbf{x}*\mathbf{y})/\mathbf{y}, \ \mathbf{x} \rightarrow (\mathbf{y}*\mathbf{x})\backslash\mathbf{y}$$

– informally, any category $\mathbf{x}$ can have a form in which it can forwards-combine with any category $\mathbf{y}$ to form a product $(\mathbf{x}*\mathbf{y})$, or backwards-combine with any category $\mathbf{y}$ to form a product $(\mathbf{y}*\mathbf{x})$ – and

$$(\mathbf{x}/\mathbf{y})/\mathbf{z} \rightarrow \mathbf{x}/(\mathbf{z}*\mathbf{y}), \ \mathbf{x}/(\mathbf{z}*\mathbf{y}) \rightarrow (\mathbf{x}/\mathbf{y})/\mathbf{z}$$

– that is, a functor taking two arguments in a nested fashion, one after the other in two separate operations of function application, can instead take the product of the two in a single operation. For example, the category of a ditransitive verb could be either $((S\backslash NP)/NP_{ben})/NP_{acc}$, as in 4.8 above, or $(S\backslash NP)/(NP_{acc}*NP_{ben})$, giving the derivation

4.13 Chris   gave   <u>a fish</u> <u>to Tigger</u>
        NP $(S\backslash NP)/(NP_{acc}*NP_{ben})$ NP_{acc} NP_{ben}

$$\begin{array}{c} \overline{} \\ NP_{acc}*NP_{ben} \end{array}$$

$$\frac{}{S\backslash NP} {>}A$$

$$\frac{}{S} {<}A$$

Manipulating a function into a form where it takes only one argument at a time is known as 'currying', after the logician who proved it could always be done; this inverse process is sometimes called 'un-currying' (see Oehrle (1987: 213) for further references and discussion).

From an algebraic viewpoint, products and the operations which depend on them are entirely natural, yet they have been little known, and not at all used, in categorial natural language description until very recently. Oehrle (1987) introduces Cartesian NP × NP products (without comment: 1987: 209) as part of the basis for his account of gapping (see Ch.5.iii.c). They were re-invented in Wood (1986, more fully developed as Wood 1989) to simplify the description of non-constituent co-ordination, especially in ditransitive constructions (see 4.13 above, and Ch.5.iii.d). In Bouma (1989) they give a structurally complete system, returning left-branching derivations, without the use of composition and raising, and thus without spurious ambiguity in parsing. Thus they are at least becoming more widely recognized, although it remains to be seen how popular they will become in use.

All the connectives, and binary rules, suggested so far are subject to the condition of 'adjacency': a functor can only apply to an argument directly adjacent to it. This has the effect of constraining word order, as is necessary – the grammar must not be able to accept *Chris the fed cat* by letting the determiner apply to its noun argument across the intervening verb – but for the same reason it cannot accept grammatical instances of discontinuous constituents. Some proposed extensions of the rule set beyond adjacency will be discussed below.

There are also proposals for new 'non-concatenative' connectives, mainly suggested by Moortgat (e.g. Moortgat 1988b: 108ff.), which are not bounded by adjacency, and which thereby go beyond the power of the Lambek calculus. The 'extraction' operator ↑ ('up arrow') can be read as 'gap' – $A{\uparrow}C$ (A gap C) will form A if it can find C, not necessarily adjacent, but somewhere in the string being analysed. Or, put somewhat differently, $A{\uparrow}C$ is the result of removing one occurrence of an element of type C from an element of type A. (This bears an obvious similarity to the GPSG 'slash' feature for gaps.) The inverse 'infixation' operator ↓ ('down arrow', 'infix') looks not for a gap but for a landing site: $A{\downarrow}B$ is assigned to an element which will form A by being infixed anywhere in the string B. (The up and down arrows of LFG, typographically identical, are not related; the double-shafted arrow 'meta-variables' used for long-distance dependency relations are at least superficially similar.)

Technically, complex categories formed with these connectives are not functions but relations, as they return more than one valid result for any given argument. Two specialized forms of particular linguistic interest are '**A** > **B** and **B** < **A**, which are interpreted as right infixation before the last, and left-infixation after the first element of the argument type, respectively' (Moortgat 1988b: 110): these make it possible to describe a number of syntactic and morphological phenomena, including 'verb-second' word order in German.

Moortgat's reason for preferring more powerful connectives to more powerful rules for describing the same limited phenomena is that rules, once introduced, can apply anywhere. They will thus over-generate unless constrained by *ad hoc* stipulations, artificial limitations on the free algebra of the system; and the linguistic validity of a free algebra is one of the main attractions of a CG. Connectives will occur only in lexically assigned categories, so arbitrary stipulation will be confined to the lexicon, which is its proper domain.

4.iii EXTENDING THE SET OF RULES

One might suspect the Lambek calculus of holding a purely arbitrary – even if convenient – point on the wide scale of complexity and power, but, as we have seen, there is some defence against this charge. Lambek himself is prepared to describe his system as a 'calculus' only because it is a deductive system, with specified axioms and rules of inference, from which a number of rules are provable, not all of which are actually used in categorial linguistic description. Recall his comment in a footnote that 'The calculus presented here is formally identical with a calculus constructed ... for a discussion of canonical mappings in linear and multilinear algebra' (1958 [1988]: 171). From a logical perspective, Moortgat argues that it is 'analogous to the implicational fragment of propositional logic' (1988b: 27ff.).

It is not, however, adequate for natural language description. In particular, although it offers structural completeness in the description of continuous strings and substrings, it has, as we have seen, no way of dealing with the original bug-bear, discontinuous constituents. These have been the focus of a great part of recent work in CG, and the motivation for many of the proposed extensions to Lambek's system (L). The difficulty is to extend the system just far enough, without allowing wild overgeneration. Rules which allow some sort of permutation risk collapsing into total 'permutation closure', licensing any possible order of elements (thus LP). Rules which allow deletion ('contraction') or copying ('expansion') (thus LPCE) are comparably profligate. The problem is how to define a system at the appropriate level between L and LPCE (see Moortgat 1988b: 45, 46, etc.), but without resorting to *ad hoc*, externally stipulated constraints, preserving the 'free algebra'. Moortgat, as we have seen, uses specialized connectives, lexically assigned and constrained, but most proposals have focused on the set of rules, mainly binary, syntagmatic rules.

There are three directions for extension of Lambek's set of rules: through recursive power, freedom in directionality and/or permutation and the acceptance of contraction and expansion, that is, allowing a function to apply to an argument more or less than once. Each of these has been put to use, and will be illustrated here. Recursion underlies the 'generalized composition' with which Ades and Steedman (1982) treat unbounded dependencies. Directional variants have been proposed for most combination rules, as have new rules of permutation or 'wrapping', to handle other discontinuities and word-order variations. Various forms of contraction and expansion allow for gaps and multiple dependencies.

A word of warning is in order. The rules which make up the Lambek calculus were designed to form one complete system: the same is not true for the proposals discussed in this chapter. Almost all have been made independently of each other, motivated by different linguistic (and/or formal or computational) phenomena, and taking different positions on any number of trade-offs; some, indeed, have been developed explicitly as mutually exclusive alternative analyses of the same data. Thus although the sum total of these developments, and the total coverage of the specific linguistic descriptions to be described in the next chapter, may seem impressive, they do not add up to their apparent total. Some are deliberate counters to others; some are, often by luck, compatible, but generally ignore each other. A single CG which incorporated all these extensions, even one which avoided internal contradictions, would be far too large, complex and cumbersome for real use, a long way from the elegant simplicity of the original 'core' grammar. This is one of the greatest problems facing CGs at the moment: the need for this lively, rapidly expanding body of work to recover in its practices the coherence of its shared underlying principles.

4.iii.a Recursion

Recursion can appear in a grammar in many ways, with different effects on its weak and strong generative capacity and formal power. Two have been discussed already. Raising allows infinitely many derivations for the same string, by allowing a functor and its argument to be alternately raised, leap-frogging each other, although the rest of the derivational pattern is unaffected. Division together with composition has more drastic effects, giving the grammar structural completeness. The third and most powerful recursive rule to have gained some currency — and the only binary recursive rule — is generalized composition, the form of composition found most notably in Ades and Steedman (1982), which gives a grammar full context-sensitive power.

In the discussion of the basic binary rule of function composition above (Ch.3.iii) it was observed that 'Partial Combination' as formulated in Ades and Steedman (1982) licensed both simple and generalized composition. After some discussion (1982: 554, fn. 7) they adopt the formulation

$$X\$/Y_S \ Y\$'/Z_S \rightarrow X\$\$'/Z_S$$

under the convention that **X\$** is a variable ranging over the set which includes **X** and all functions into **X**, comparably **Y\$'**; the **\$** and **\$'** symbols thus denote the remainders (if any) of the categories. Carrying forward the remainder in **X\$** does not affect the power of the rule, but consuming **Y** while leaving **\$'** does, allowing both the simple reduction **A/(B/C) (B/C)/D → A/D** and the generalized **A/B (B/C)/D → A/C/D**. (According to one common convention, complex categories are taken to be left-associative unless specified otherwise — **A/B/C** is equivalent to **(A/B)/C** — so generalized composition is sometimes referred to as 'parenthesis-free'.)

Although simple composition is enough to permit an incremental derivation, as Ades and Steedman wish, in most cases, its generalized power is needed for such derivations as 4.14 or 4.15 (notation very slightly adapted):

4.14 Who do you think   loves   him?
    NP   S|S   (S|NP)|NP   NP
          ————————————————>GC
             (S|NP)|NP
  ————————————————————————<A
    S|NP
  ————————————————————————————>A
            S

(ibid.: 546)

4.15

```
Who  did you      give        the book that you bought for Mary?
NP   S|VP (VP|NP)|NP                        NP
        ───────────────── >GC
            (S|NP)|NP
     ─────────────────────── <A
       S|NP
     ─────────────────────────────────────────────────── >A
                             S
```

(ibid.: 554, fn. 7)

(Note the unusual position, taken consistently in this paper, that the object argument is incorporated after the subject: on most accounts, this derivation would give incorrect semantic bindings for subject and object (see also Ch.5.iii below). Composition into **NP** is blocked by stipulation, to prevent overgeneration of extraction to such examples as *This man I burned a book about* (ibid.: 545).)

However, it was suspected at the time that generalized composition 'almost certainly induces a grammar which is no longer strictly C[ontext] F[ree]' (ibid.). The suspicion was confirmed and a formal proof provided by Joyce Friedman (Friedman *et al.* 1986; Friedman and Venkatesan 1986). Informally, it can be shown that it is generalized composition which can generate context-sensitive languages, because the result of composing two functions can be more complex than either original function, as when composing $X|A\ A|Y \rightarrow X|Y$ where **A** is atomic and **X** and **Y** are complex. Steedman (1990: 215, fn.10) mentions a slightly different proof by Weir (1988) to the same effect, and (ibid.: 218–19, also 258, fn. 43) now proposes a restricted generalized rule for English, to a depth bounded by the maximum valency in the lexicon, but suggests that the fully general form is likely still to be needed for the analysis of Dutch crossed dependencies (see Ch.5.iii.c).

Generalized composition is seldom used elsewhere, but its use and subsequent formal analysis have been influential; its excessive formal power has motivated a number of the trade-offs between binary and unary rules or between restrictions on rules and on lexical assignment which characterize recent categorial research. For example, Uszkoreit (1986) and Zeevat (1988), as mentioned above, reject composition; Bouma (1989) re-institutes Lambek's product connective in order to do without any form of composition; Wood (1989) keeps simple composition, but by the use of products can do without the generalized form. Attempts to restrict generalized composition, not inherently, but by annotations on the form of the rule (such as the constraint against composition into NP mentioned above) were the stimulus for Moortgat's shift to the use of specialized connectives in lexically assigned categories, keeping arbitrary stipulation within the lexicon. And a good deal of formal work, such as that by Friedman and by Weir just referred to, having established the context-sensitive power of the full recursive generalization of function composition, has gone on to explore in valuable ways the possible space of 'mildly context-sensitive' CGs.

4.iii.b Permutation

The second general way in which the Lambek calculus can be extended to handle a wider range of linguistic phenomena is through the introduction of some device(s) to deal with variable word order and discontinuity, and a number of different proposals have been made for this. As a linguistic issue, these proposals and the differences among them will be discussed more fully below (Ch.6.iv), but for the moment a brief, slightly more abstract and formal account is appropriate.

The earliest CGs were non-directional, imposing no constraints – and giving no information – on word order. This is because they were semantic systems, to which surface word order was irrelevant: both Bar-Hillel and Lambek, in introducing CGs for serious syntactic description, imposed directionality on the slash connectives in complex categories. It remained useful, as we have seen, to have a neutral slash, both for use in abstract rule schemata and to encode some simple cases of variable word order, such as the position of English sentence-modifying adverbs at either the beginning or end of a sentence (see 4.11, 4.12 above). One critical limitation on this freedom is that categories must still be adjacent in order to combine – it does not yet give us an answer to the problem of discontinuous 'constituents'.

One pattern found particularly often in both syntax and morphology, across a wide range of languages, involves some element – often a clitic or auxiliary – occurring in either second or penultimate position in a phrase or sentence ('Wackernagel's Law': see Bach 1984: 14–15 for examples from Amharic and Xa'isla (Kwakiutl) as well as the more familiar Germanic verb-second constraints). Emmon Bach, in a series of papers starting in 1979 (e.g. Bach 1979a, 1979b, 1984), suggested the use of 'wrapping' rules (formalized as RWRAP and LWRAP) to describe this phenomenon. These should not be confused with movement rules in a transformational grammar: they are function/argument rules like any other, except that they are not restricted to adjacent elements (see Ch.6.ii below). Formally,

(1) RCON: 'Right-Concatenation' (a/b)
   If **a** is the function and **b** the argument, then RCON(a,b) is **a__b**.
(2) LCON: 'Left-Concatenation' (b\a$_{[L]}$)
   If **a** is the function and **b** the argument, then LCON(a,b) is **b__a**.
(3) RWRAP: 'Right-Wrap'
   (i) If **a** is simple, then RWRAP(a,b) = RCON(a,b).
   (ii) If **a** has the form [$_{XP}$ **X W**], then RWRAP(a,b) is **X__b__W**.
(4) PREPCON: 'Preposition Concatenation'
   If **a** has the form **A Prep** (where **A** is any category), then PREPCON(a,b) is **A__**[$_{PP}$ **Prep b**].

(Bach 1979b: 516)

Thus

(5) a. RCON: try to go, present employer, the men, see Bill
   b. LCON: walk slowly, man in the street, man here
   c. RWRAP: persuade Bill to leave, easy man to please, too hot to eat
   d. PREPCON: depend on Mary, arrive at the decision, proud of his children, angry at Bill

(ibid.)

RWRAP ((persuade to go), John) = (persuade John to go)

(Bach 1984: 9)

Bach (1979b) looks at the use of RWRAP, in particular, in describing control constructions (see Ch.5.iii.b below), and suggests (1984) a wrapping analysis of Dutch complement structures with intersecting dependencies. This approach is developed further in Hoeksema and Janda's (1988) proposals for categorial morphology (see Ch.5.ii below). Moortgat (characteristically), as we have seen (Ch.4.ii), introduces not a rule but a lexically restricted connective which dictates the right behaviour.

More general and powerful are the directional variants of basic rules such as composition and raising. 'Disharmonic' composition, for example, combines two functors with slashes looking in different directions:

$$X/Y_S \; Y\backslash Z_S \rightarrow X\backslash Z_S \text{ (forward crossing composition)}$$
$$Y/Z_S \; X\backslash Y_S \rightarrow X/Z_S \text{ (backward crossing composition)}$$

The backward rule is central to Moortgat's (1988a) analysis of discontinuous dependencies and bracketing paradoxes in morphology; he restricts it through lexical restrictions on type-shifting, with interesting consequences for autonomous lexicalism. It turns up again in Morrill's (1987) account of right extraposition, and in Steedman's (1987: 420) account of subcategorized adverbials, where it is linked to the raising of PPs over their VPs:

4.16 (books)   which   I will   put   on the table
        (N\N)/(S/NP) S/VP (VP/PP)/NP VP\(VP/PP)
                                    ——————————————————<XC
                                        VP/NP
                        ——————————————————————>C
                                    S/NP
        ————————————————————————————>A
                        N\N

The forward rule – like the backward version, heavily constrained by annotations – is used in Steedman's analysis of gapping, and will be discussed further in due course (Ch.5.iii.c). Comparable directional variants have been suggested for raising – see Steedman (1991a).

It is clear that disharmonic rules overgenerate. Indeed, formally, they immediately collapse the system into permutation closure – that is, any word order will be accepted (for a formal proof of this, see Moortgat 1988b: 90ff.). The debate is still very much open as to how best to define an algebraically clean grammar which allows usefully more freedom than the Lambek calculus, but less than the total freedom of unconstrained permutation.

4.iii.c Contraction and expansion

Even a full LP grammar (the Lambek calculus extended by unrestrained permutation rules) has a strict 'count' property – every function must apply to every argument specified in its category once and only once. An intransitive verb must occur with exactly one noun phrase, a transitive verb with exactly two and so on. Rules of contraction and expansion remove even this restriction: a contraction rule allows a functor looking for two arguments of the same type to be satisfied with one, an expansion rule allows a functor looking for only one argument to apply to two. Van Benthem (1987a) gives schematic forms for these 'structural rules':

$$\text{Contraction: } \mathbf{U,X} \rightarrow \mathbf{Y} \text{ if } \mathbf{U,X,X} \rightarrow \mathbf{Y}$$
$$\text{Expansion: } \mathbf{U,X,X} \rightarrow \mathbf{Y} \text{ if } \mathbf{U,X} \rightarrow \mathbf{Y}$$

Unconstrained, such rules would overgenerate wildly. There are some linguistic phenomena, however, for which they seem appropriate. Expansion rules (together with some form of permutation) can handle 'copying' (Ross 1967) constructions such as 'Right Dislocation' (*Chris gives them dog-biscuits, the stray cats which come over the garden wall*), where the verb finds its syntactic indirect object in the pronoun *them* but must apply again to the 'dislocated' full NP which provides the semantic content. Contraction offers an approach to gapping, where two elements should be present but one does duty for both (*Michael fed Tigger, and Chris the neighbours' cat*).

One detailed proposal with the effect of contraction is the treatment of parasitic gaps in Steedman (1987) and Szabolcsi (1987). In a construction like *articles which I will file without reading*, the phrase *file without reading* displays much of the behaviour of a transitive verb, which suggests that it should have the category **VP/NP**. This assignment can be derived using Szabolcsi's rule of 'functional connection', Steedman's (1988: 425–6) 'substitution':

$$\text{Y}/\text{Z}_S \ (\text{X}\backslash\text{Y})/\text{Z}_S \rightarrow \text{X}/\text{Z}_S$$

and thus

4.17   file   <u>without reading</u>
    VP/NP   (VP\VP)/NP
    ————————————S
        VP/NP

This will be discussed in more detail below (Ch.5.iii.c). Even among the many categorial accounts of gapping constructions, however, as we will see, rule types with this much scope for overgeneration tend to be avoided, and are probably more important in defining the end of a formal spectrum of possibilities than in practical natural language description: it is characteristic that the thorough discussion in Morrill *et al.* (1990), although linguistically sensitive and valuable, is cast primarily in the terms and notation of logical proof.

4.iv COMBINATORY CATEGORIAL GRAMMAR

The range of possible categorial calculi is very wide, and it is not surprising that a good deal of effort has gone into motivating the various exact points along that range which different categorial grammarians have adopted. This can be done by appealing to a number of different independent criteria. The Lambek calculus, L, as we have seen, is a deductive system, shown by Lambek to coincide with an independently justified algebraic calculus, and by Moortgat to correspond to 'the implicational fragment of propositional logic' (see Ch.4.iii above). Systems less powerful than L are commonly defended on grounds of their constrained formal power and/or greater computational tractability. Extensions to L are justified by the need to describe awkward linguistic phenomena such as discontinuous constituency, non-constituent co-ordination, and the (in)famous, provably context-sensitive cross-serial dependencies in Dutch embedded clauses (see Ch.5.iii.c below). Or one can move away from L altogether to different systems which retain L's virtues in a framework more appropriate for natural language analysis.

One approach which respects both formal and linguistic considerations is that of Combinatory Categorial Grammar (CCG), first proposed by Steedman and Szabolcsi at the Tucson conference in 1985, in what was eventually published as Steedman (1988). Questioning what operations really do have to be added to a minimal Ajdukiewicz grammar for adequate natural language description, not just *ad hoc* for some given language(s) but responsive to fundamental language ‾universals, Steedman (1988: 417–18) suggests that

> the operations that we have to add bear a striking resemblance to the 'combinators' which Curry and Feys (1958) use to define the foundations of the lambda calculus and all applicative systems – that is, systems expressing the operations of functional application and abstraction.

Curry's most basic original set of combinators consisted of four, **B**, **C**, **W** and **I**; slightly later introductions are **S** and **K**. They can be explained as follows:

B: functional composition

$$\text{semantics: } \mathbf{B}FG = \lambda x[F(Gx)]$$

C: commutation, 'which maps two-argument functions such as **(X/Y)/Z** onto the corresponding function **(X/Z)/Y** with the arguments reversed' (ibid.: 431), thus a permutation rule

$$\text{semantics: } \mathbf{C}F = \lambda x[\lambda y[Fyx]]$$

W: doubling, 'takes a function of two arguments to a function of one argument which identifies the two arguments' (ibid.: 432), thus possibly related to such phenomena as 'Equi-NP Deletion' (Steedman) or reflexivization (Oehrle)

$$\text{semantics: } \mathbf{W}F = \lambda x[Fxx]$$

I: identity

$$\text{semantics: } \mathbf{I}x = x$$

S: substitution (see 4.iii.c above; similar to **W**; an alternative possible rule for Equi)

$$\text{semantics: } \mathbf{S}FG = \lambda x[Fx(Gx)]$$

K: cancelling

$$\text{semantics: } \mathbf{K}xy = x$$

Almost all the rules needed for the description of natural language, it is claimed, can be naturally expressed using only the 'basic' combinators **B**, **C**, **W** and **S**, and compositions of these to define further combinatory operations. The body of Steedman's paper argues, mainly from English constructions involving single and multiple dependencies, that the range of this formally motivated system corresponds persuasively to the range of rules suggested by linguistic evidence and intuition (the reader is referred to the original for details). It is further argued that it also corresponds suggestively to the range of operations used, for efficiency reasons, in compilers for applicative or functional programming languages (ibid.: 417–18):

> Crucially, combinators allow the process of abstraction to be defined without invoking bound variables. The striking parallel between the particular set of combinators that is implicit in the grammar of English (and, by implication, other languages), and the systems of combinators that are used in certain highly efficient compilers for applicative programming languages … suggests that the reason natural language grammars take this form (rather than resembling some other applicative system, such as the lambda calculus itself) may be to do with the computational advantages of avoiding the use of bound variables.

Szabolcsi (1987) develops this line, suggesting that combinators make bound variables unnecessary not only for the analysis of 'gapped' constructions but also for 'overt bound variables' such as anaphors. The issue of universality is discussed further in Steedman (1990) and will be taken up later (Ch.6.iii). A somewhat different aspect is Wittenburg's (1987) introduction of 'predictive' combinators as a solution to the spurious ambiguity problem, another issue to which we will return later (Ch.6.vi).

4.v UNIFICATION CATEGORIAL GRAMMARS

Over the past ten years or less, the whole field of theoretical linguistics has been transformed by the growing influence of computational natural language processing. One of the most important single ingredients in this has been the emergence of 'unification-based' – simple but powerful, declarative, monotonic – description formalisms. Not only implementation environments like Functional Unification Grammar (Kay 1985) and Definite Clause Grammars (Pereira and Warren 1980) but also new linguistic theories, notably Lexical-Functional Grammar (Bresnan 1982), Generalized Phrase Structure Grammar (Gazdar *et al.* 1985), and Head-driven Phrase Structure Grammar (Pollard and Sag 1987), have been informed by their use of unification, and CGs are no exception.

Unification-based formalisms are also known as 'complex-feature-based'. They encode objects, not as atomic, but as bundles of 'feature-value' or 'attribute-value' pairs, and build up descriptions of more complex objects by combining partial information from different sources – phrases, for example, from their constituent words: *the* is definite, *cat* is singular, so *the cat* must be both definite and singular. This ability easily to handle incomplete information is one of the important virtues of unification. Formally, unification is an operation of set union over sets of attribute-value pairs (except that it fails in a few situations, such as the attempt to assign two different values to the same variable (see 4.20, 4.22 below), where union could apply). Thus the known formal properties of sets apply, a valuable mathematical foundation.

It is conventional to write feature-value specifications in square brackets, each feature followed by its value, a format which may be familiar from its use in LFG:

4.18
$$\begin{bmatrix} \text{number:} & \text{singular} \\ \text{person:} & \text{third} \end{bmatrix}$$

A complex description like this can itself be the value of a feature inside a more complex description:

4.19
$$\begin{bmatrix} \text{cat:} & \text{NP} \\ \text{agreement:} & \begin{bmatrix} \text{number:} & \text{singular} \\ \text{person:} & \text{third} \end{bmatrix} \end{bmatrix}$$

Two partial descriptions can be unified as long as no features are given conflicting values:

4.20
$$\begin{bmatrix} \text{cat:} & \text{NP} \\ \text{agreement:} & \text{[number: singular]} \end{bmatrix}$$

unifies with

4.21
$$\begin{bmatrix} \text{cat:} & \text{NP} \\ \text{agreement:} & \text{[person: third]} \end{bmatrix}$$

to give 4.19, but 4.20 cannot unify with

4.22
$$\begin{bmatrix} \text{cat:} & \text{NP} \\ \text{agreement:} & \text{[number: plural]} \end{bmatrix}$$

There is, of course, more to it than this: this should, however, be enough background for an outline of the encodings of CG principles in a unification environment which are known as Unification Categorial Grammar (UCG) and Categorial Unification Grammar (CUG).

The two names, UCG and CUG, distinguish two different workings-out of the same ideas, which appear to have arisen at about the same time but (initially) independently of each other. Uszkoreit (1986: 187) proposed CUGs as a formalism to 'embody the essential properties of both unification and CG formalisms'. Zeevat *et al.* (1987) and Zeevat (1988) present UCG as a CG enriched by insights from Shieber's computational work on unification. Uszkoreit's plural is significant: CUGs are presented as a general framework, a wide space in which variation is available between different grammars, while UCG is a specific individual theory.

Uszkoreit sets out the central insight in very general terms. Basic categories have a feature for 'category' (the 'graph' notation of the original is here translated into the simpler, more conventional form):

4.23 [cat: N]
      [cat: S]

and may have additional features for finer-grained information:

$$4.24 \quad \begin{bmatrix} \text{cat:} & \text{N} & \\ \text{agr:} & \begin{bmatrix} \text{pers:} & 3 \\ \text{num:} & \text{Sg} \end{bmatrix} \end{bmatrix}$$

$$\begin{bmatrix} \text{cat:} & \text{S} \\ \text{form:} & \text{Finite} \end{bmatrix}$$

Indeed, one of the appeals of a complex-feature-based formalism for CGs is its ability to encode in a uniform way this sort of more delicate information, which in the classical notation takes the form of cumbersome sub- or superscript annotations or (probably in part for that very reason) is ignored.

The information content of complex categories can be given in the same way, defined at the top level by the three features 'value', 'direction' and 'argument': thus the intransitive verb category S\NP becomes

$$4.25 \quad \begin{bmatrix} \text{val:} & \text{S} \\ \text{dir:} & \text{Left} \\ \text{arg:} & \text{NP} \end{bmatrix}$$

Again, additional features can readily be added to ensure subject–verb agreement and so on.

4.26
$$
\begin{bmatrix}
\text{val:} & \begin{bmatrix} \text{cat:} & \text{S} \\ \text{form:} & \text{Finite} \end{bmatrix} \\
\text{dir:} & \text{Left} \\
\text{arg:} & \begin{bmatrix} \text{cat:} & \text{NP} \\ \text{agr:} & \begin{bmatrix} \text{pers:} & 3 \\ \text{num:} & \text{Sg} \end{bmatrix} \end{bmatrix}
\end{bmatrix}
$$

This particular line has been followed mainly by computational linguists working with Shieber's (1984) PATR-II grammar development system (see also, for example, Karttunen 1987, 1989).

Zeevat *et al.* are more specific: UCG is a grammar, not a space of possible grammars. A category or 'sign' contains four major attributes: phonology (W), syntactic category (C), semantics (S) and order (O), written either as a vertical list or as a sequence separated by colons. Phonology, when not centrally at issue, is commonly represented by orthography. Syntactic categories take the conventional form, except for the factoring out of the order specification; **S**, **N** and **NP** are atomic, but may be marked with mainly morphological feature specifications similar to those of GPSG. The semantic system is based on Discourse Representation Theory (see further Ch.6.i below), observing compositionality. Order has the two possible values 'pre' and 'post': an argument marked 'pre' needs its functor to precede it; an argument marked 'post' has its functor following. Any of these attributes may be uninstantiated, its place held by a variable.

Thus, for example (Zeevat 1988: 208–9), a lexical entry for the verb *dance*, a function to a finite sentence from a nominative NP, might be

4.27 W: dances
    C: sent [fin] /np [nom] :x:pre
    S: [e] DANCE(e,x)
    O:

The NP subject at this point is marked, wrongly, to take a preceding functor; this will eventually be reversed (see below). The proper noun *Harry*, of itself indifferent as to case or order, might be

4.28 W: harry
    C: np
    S: HARRY
    O:

and the general description of any subject NP abstracts away from

phonology and semantics, but specifies nominative case and that its
functor should precede it, corresponding with the specification on the
verb above:

4.29 W:
    C: np [nom]
    S:
    O: pre

By unifying 4.28 with 4.29 we get a description of *Harry* acting as subject of some sentence:

4.30 W: harry
    C: np [nom]
    S: HARRY
    O: pre

This in turn can unify with the lexical entry for *dances* (4.27) to
describe *Harry dances*:

4.31 W: dances
    C: sent [fin] /harry:np [nom] :HARRY:pre
    S: [e] DANCE(e,HARRY)
    O:

There is one remaining problem: the order attribute says that the argument should be preceded by its functor, so we in fact have a description of *dances Harry*. When the subject is type-raised – for
independent semantic reasons – its functor–argument relation with
the verb is reversed. The original lexical entry for the verb specified
that its subject should *have* a preceding functor; this is inherited by
the raised subject, which *is* a preceding functor. This somewhat
counter-intuitive description of word order was dictated partly by the
fact that, since the order specification is interpreted in terms of
function–argument relations, its significance will vary depending on
whether a particular nominal is raised or not; therefore the only safe
place to specify order is on the verb. There are also contributing limitations in the computational environment used (a simple PATR
system: see Shieber 1984, 1987), and more elegant solutions could be
imagined, though none have as yet been implemented (Zeevat, p.c.).
    The set of attributes is somewhat different in the broadly similar
system used by Whitelock (1988) to describe the morpho-syntax of

Japanese. 'phon' describes phonology; 'morpho-syntax' is a set of features, 'subcat' holds a list of items subcategorized for and 'cat' gives the syntactic category. Rather than defining this with a single feature 'arg' whose value must be a sign and a feature 'dir' whose possible values are atomic 'right' and 'left' (or 'pre' and 'post'), 'cat' is a set of three features, 'left', 'right' and 'result', all with signs as their values. The separation of morpho-syntactic features from complex categories increases the expressive power of the grammar, and in Whitelock's analysis 'certain functors define their arguments in terms of morpho-syntactic features, and others define them in terms of their complex categories' (1988: 235).

The use of variables as feature values in categories is obviously tied closely to the use of unification to instantiate them. Moortgat (1988b) comments on the connection in logical terms; Zeevat (1988) explores it from a more linguistic point of view, and uses it to give an account of crossed dependencies in Dutch infinitival groups which avoids the use of functional composition. Calder *et al.* (1989) outline the use of UCG for natural language generation. A unification-based Combinatory CG is suggested by Steedman (1991a).

Unification-based formalisms offer greater linguistic expressiveness than classical CGs, in a clear and well-founded way. The main concern is that they are so general that the expressiveness may be too great. There are no inherent constraints on what may stand as an attribute or a legal value (as the two different treatments of word order just mentioned illustrate). The best defence is probably that there are no obvious inherent constraints on what may turn out to be linguistically relevant and in need of description, so it is a positive virtue to use a formalism which can encode in a uniform way whatever may come along. But it is easy to be profligate in such a system, and one of CG's traditional virtues has been parsimony. New attributes and values deserve to be treated with the same scepticism as new atomic categories; the ease of expanding categorial linguistic description to include an ever wider range of aspects of language in ever finer detail is a powerful stimulus to growth, but must not be allowed to lead to Byzantine efflorescence.

FURTHER READING

For the formal and linguistic properties of categorial calculi beyond L, see (again) Moortgat (1988b), to which my debt in this and the previous chapter is considerable.

The seminal and most easily available source for CCG is Steedman

(1988). For UCG/CUG, Shieber (1986) is an excellent, much fuller introduction to both the formal and linguistic aspects of unification and of the principal grammar formalisms which use it (although CGs are not included). The Introduction to Reyle and Rohrer (1988) and Chapter 2 of Pollard and Sag (1987) are also helpful. The most accessible primary source for UCG is Zeevat (1988); Uszkoreit (1986) and Karttunen (1989) also give clear introductions to the basic ideas of CUG. More specialized examples of linguistic description in both paradigms are appearing too quickly to keep track of: watch in particular the proceedings of the annual meetings of the Association for Computational Linguistics, of the biennial meetings of its European Chapter, and of the biennial international Coling conferences.

5 Current practice

The principles and devices of CGs, with some idea of their linguistic motivation and application, should now be reasonably clear. The aim of this chapter is to change perspective, and survey a range of linguistic phenomena and some ways in which they have been described using CGs.

This is not as simple as it sounds. CG is an increasingly lively research field, in which new work is appearing faster than one can hope to keep up with it, but for the most part in specialist conference proceedings, working papers or even less accessible formats. Including dissertations, technical reports and privately circulated manuscripts, I know of work on (at least) anaphoric binding, auxiliary verbs, causatives, clitics, co-ordination, grammatical relations, inflexional morphology, intonation, long-distance dependency, modifiers and specifiers, nominal compounding, parasitic gaps, passives, raising, reflexives, relative clauses, switch reference, synthetic compounding, verb gapping and word order, and on Dutch, Dyrbal, English, Finnish, French, German, Hopi, Icelandic, Italian, Japanese, Korean, Luiseño, Malagasy, Maori, Russian, Spanish, Tairora, Turkish and Warlpiri. There is undoubtedly more of which I am not aware.

After the selection problem comes the (in)coherence problem. The comments above (Ch. 4.iii) on the diversity and frequent incompatibility of proposed extensions to the rule system apply even more strongly here. Even CGs proper, as we have seen, take in a wide range of grammars, with different sorts and degrees of complexity in different areas, leading naturally to very different accounts of the same linguistic phenomena. If one allows the whole broader enterprise of general type theory, the diversity is even greater. On some topics there are articulated lines of argument, where some proposals explicitly build on or reply to others. In many cases there are simply collections of unrelated suggestions. To impose a coherent cover on these cans of worms would be to misrepresent the present character of the categorial enterprise: the reader is asked to accept that much of what follows will have far more the flavour of a grab-bag than of a boxed selection.

The organization will be familiar: phonology (sparsely represented), then inflexional and derivational morphology (the former even sparser, the latter rather better represented), then a number of the most debated topics in syntax – passives, raising and control, unbounded, discontinuous and multiple dependencies, co-ordination and gapping. Categorial investigation has focused on syntax and its relation to semantics, and on the 'non-canonical' constructions which seemed to spell its doom in the early days, such as discontinuous constituents and non-constituent co-ordination, leaving gaps in the 'core grammar': it will be a sign of real maturity when more concern shifts to providing integrated broader coverage of whole languages and families.

Given the centrality of semantics in CG, it may appear strange that there is no 'Semantics' section in this chapter. The reason is that, although it is a central general issue, and most syntactic proposals come with integral semantic interpretations, there has not been that much work on particular topics in semantics. More has been done in the wider type-theoretic school than in 'pure' CG – there is substantial work on quantification, in particular – but it lies beyond my present scope. The general issues are discussed in Ch.6.i.

5.i PHONOLOGY

Given the informing reductionism of CGs, their concentration on using and describing only what is essential, it is in a way surprising that so little attention has been paid to the inescapably essential level of phonology. Moortgat recognizes its importance – 'The level of autonomous syntax turns out to be a dispensable artefact between the two indispensable levels of sound and meaning' (1988b: 60) – but is one of the few to give it any sort of consideration, looking at prosody and phrasing. Oehrle (1981) discusses constructions like vocative and appositive phrases whose analysis depends on intonational characteristics. Wheeler (1988) looks at Russian phonology, Steedman (1991b) at intonation. UCG takes phonology more seriously than do classical CGs, although even there it is common for orthography to stand duty for true phonological analysis.

Moortgat's interest is in the mismatches between syntax and prosody, and their treatment in a Lambek-based calculus. The structural completeness of L makes the notion of syntactic constituent structure vacuous, but the prosodic structure of a string is empirically observable, and it is this which can be directly interpreted semantically. Moortgat gives a compositional phonological interpretation procedure to assign prosodic phrasings to derivations in Gentzen sequent calculus. The basic phonological operator is one of concatenation, which is neither associative nor commutative; that is, grouping and order are invariant. The rules used in the proof procedure are linked with rules in the phonological algebra. Syntactic and morphological 'bracketing paradoxes' – complex nominal phrases like *the lettering on the cover of the book,* where the syntactic/ semantic structure is (*the lettering (on the cover (of the book)))* but the prosodic structure is ((*the lettering*) (*on the cover*) (*of the book*)), derived nouns like *ungrammaticality* – are shown to be resolvable in this way, and it is hinted in conclusion (ibid.: 69) that by encoding the necessary information in lexical category assignments it is again possible to localize arbitrary stipulation in the lexicon.

Wheeler (1988), starting from basic principles and applying them to a careful analysis of significant data, 'address[es] the question of what a phonological component would be like which is compatible with the basic tenets of categorial theories ... as a case study, focus[ing] on the analysis of final devoicing and voicing assimilation in Russian' (1988: 467). Rather than the basically transformational character of standard generative phonology, Wheeler suggests, a categorial phonology will follow the same two general principles as a categorial semantics, compositionality and invariance (or monotonicity): the interpretation of the whole is a function of the interpretation of the parts, and values once specified may not subsequently be changed (although they may initially be underspecified, and filled in later). Specifically, phonological segments will be assigned atomic or functional categories which encode the phonotactic constraints of any given language. The atomic categories are N (Nucleus, assigned to vowels) and S (Syllable). Syllable-final consonants in the general case are $N\backslash N$, initial consonants are S/N; the set of combination rules is restricted to function application, forwards and backwards. From this simple basis a convincing account is worked out of Russian voicing phenomena. Her conclusion shows that the behaviour of a segment is determined by its category, and thus implicitly (again) that the lexicon, not a separate system of rules, is the locus for restrictive stipulation.

Steedman (1991b) also explores the relation between intonation, category assignment, and 'derivational constituency'. There is no separate level of intonation structure: the level of surface structure, he argues, is also the level of both intonation structure and information structure. The flexible 'constituency' which allows the description of 'non-constituent co-ordination' (see Ch. 5.iii.d below) should not be called 'spurious' ambiguity, as the range of possible groupings within a string will correspond to a range of different intonation contours, each reflecting a different information structure. Pitch accents are defined as 'functions over boundary tones into the two major informational types, theme and rheme, where the latter category is itself a function Utterance|Theme from themes into utterances' (1991b: 278). Prosodic categories can combine by application or a very restricted form of composition. A sentence like *Fred ate the beans* has two natural intonation contours, with different derivation paths reflecting the different information structures (see the original for details of the notation for pitch accents in lines 2 and 4, and indeed of the whole analysis):

5.1

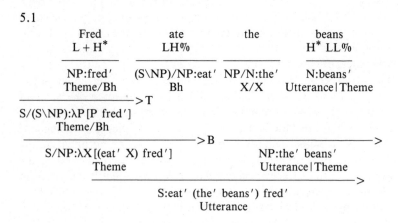

5.2

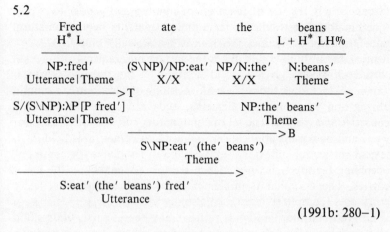

(1991b: 280–1)

In UCG, as we have seen, phonology is the first of the four basic attributes which make up the specification of any 'sign'. In many cases its value is filled by simple orthography, but it is significant that it should be there at all; some interesting work is being done in association with the central UCG enterprise (e.g. Bird and Klein 1990; Bird 1991), and should soon be ready for more general exposure. Overall, categorial phonology is beginning to gather momentum, but has a long way to go to catch up with the more traditional CG concerns of syntax and semantics.

5.ii MORPHOLOGY

CG discussions of inflexional morphology are even sparser than categorial phonology: almost nothing worth comment is easily accessible. The need for some formalization of the linguistic information commonly carried by inflexion – number and case, tense and aspect – has been acknowledged at least since Lambek, and the basic principle that inflexional morphemes be treated as functors is adopted by Šaumjan (1973) and Hiż (1968). But the classical notation pays for its elegant minimalism with inadequacy in this respect: it offers no easy way to encode such fine-grained distinctions. In a unification-based formalism they can simply be included among the features, or attributes, which make up categories.

It is therefore no surprise that, apart from early work by Schmerling (1982, 1983), the little work which has been done on inflexional morphology is mainly in the UCG paradigm. Zeevat *et al.* (1987: 207–9) discuss briefly the use of features for number and gender to express 'combinatorial restrictions', including mismatches between 'natural' and 'grammatical' values (*scissors* is syntactically plural, *Mädchen* neuter), but nothing is said about the surface mechanisms of inflexion. Whitelock (1988) gives a good account of the morpho-syntax of Japanese, including the surface morphology of case, tense, adnominalizing and adverbializing elements, and verb alternations such as causative and passive. The set of combinatory rules is restricted to forward and backward application; linguistic information is held in the lexical entries for inflexional affixes, and in templates for commonly occurring feature structures, which reduce redundancy in the lexical entries. The grammar is implemented in Prolog, with each lexical entry as a (completely readable) Prolog clause.

Derivational morphology is rather better represented, understandably perhaps: affixal derivation can be described compositionally by a natural generalization of a compositional syntax. Early proposals look at the most simply syntax-like of derivational patterns, synthetic compounding (Hoeksema) and affixal adjective formation (Reichl). Moortgat tackles the harder problem of bracketing paradoxes in Dutch, German and English word formation, and their implications for the range of rules needed by a grammar; Hoeksema and Janda look in a similar way (with similar conclusions) at language-universal morphology.

Synthetic compounds – 'endocentric adjective or noun compounds whose head ... is morphologically complex, having been derived from a verb' (Selkirk 1981: 246) – *house-cleaning*, *consumer protection*, *eye-catching*, *machine-readable* – by their complex structure and free productivity sit on the boundary between morphology and syntax. They were thus hotly debated in the early days of full-blown lexical grammar in the late 1970s and early 1980s, Roeper and Siegel (1978) proposing 'lexical transformations' analogous to syntactic transformations, Selkirk (1981) and others arguing for lexical rules which would be generalized towards syntax.

For a CG there is, of course, no debate here: Hoeksema (1985) takes a conventional CG and extends it straightforwardly to describe the structure and semantics of synthetic compounds. For example, the nominalizing affixes *-ing*, *-ion*, *-ance* have the (Lambek) category $S\$\backslash N\$$, that is, they take a preceding sentence or functor-into-a-sentence, namely, a verb, and return a nominal or functor-into-a-nominal (using generalized composition, in order to carry over the 'remainders'). The affix *-er* forms nominals from nominals, $N\backslash N$ (*left-hander*); *-ed* forms adjectives from adjective–noun compounds,

N\(A\A) (*kind-hearted*). If Hoeksema's description has a serious weakness it is in fact that it is so close to syntax that to generalize it further to 'core' morphology would not be as simple as one would like.

Šaumjan and his colleagues in the (then) Soviet Union have been concerned with morphological issues for a long time, inspired, at least partly no doubt, by the inflexional and derivational richness of the Slavic languages. Soboleva (1973) outlines an 'applicative generative' model of derivational structure in Russian, describing the 'calculus of functions' which systematically relates words within 'families'. Reichl (1982), working with the same model, describes a more restricted set of data, de-adjectival abstract nouns in English, although the issues he throws light on are far from restricted:

> the theory of the parts of speech, the lexicalist-trans-formationalist controversy, the relationship between proposi-tional and lexical semantics and, from a philosophical point of view, the problem of universals, to name only the most important.
>
> (Reichl 1982: 2)

The care and detail of his description are seriously obscured by his adherence to the largely unfamiliar east European traditions of applicative grammar, and his explicit attempt to encode in a categorial notation the concepts of transformations and of 'deep structure' is out of tune with our current understanding of CGs' basic principles. It is instructive, too, to see how quickly the bare classical notation becomes encumbered with subscripts, superscripts and additional category abbreviations, giving additional information, distinguishing otherwise indistinguishable classes or just making it all a bit more legible: as a simple example (ibid.: 157; the notation is non-directional, and 'PA' stands for 'predicative adjective'), a noun like *deafness* has to be analysed in the following way:

5.3

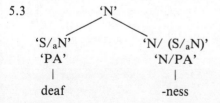

Despite all this, the thoroughness and precision of Reichl's description of a carefully chosen set of data, his awareness of alternative descriptions and his bringing back of this detail to wider issues are exemplary.

Closer in every sense is Moortgat's (1988a, 1988b) work on 'bracketing paradoxes' and discontinuous dependencies in the derivational morphology of Dutch, German and English. He proposes that such constructions can be derived by enriching the Lambek calculus with 'a mixed version of the composition rule, or equivalently, a non-harmonic version of the division rule' (Moortgat 1988a: 321). Unconstrained, as we have seen (Ch. 4.iii.b), this leads to permutation closure. To constrain it, Moortgat adopts Partee and Rooth's (1983) strategy of minimal type assignment (see Ch. 3.iv), ensuring that the more complex types produced or applied to by the disharmonic rules are governed by lexical stipulation and occur only when strictly needed.

Aronoff's 'Strong Lexicalism', the hypothesis that the lexicon is autonomous − that lexical rules (including word formation) cannot be fed by syntactic rules − is an obvious tenet for a CG. Yet certain word-formation processes, such as 'complement inheritance', appear to have phrasal semantic scope: English *believer in magic*, *indebtedness to the king*, Dutch *tevredenheid met de soep* ('the state of being happy with the soup'), *vergelijkbaar met wijn* ('comparable to wine'; ibid.: 328; 1988b: 95). At a finer grain, there are complex words and lexicalized phrases for which prosody demands one bracketing and semantics another − *ungrammaticality*, *model-theoretic*, *transformational grammarian*. These conflicts can be resolved by a flexible type-assignment system which licenses both the syntactic category needed for word-based affixation and the semantic type needed for the correct scope.

The bracketing paradoxes can be resolved within the Lambek calculus, given its structural completeness. The basic type assignments for the elements of *ungrammaticality* give the correct semantic reading, in which *un-grammatical* forms a unit which is then nominalized:

5.4 un   grammatical   ity
   A/A   A   N\A
   ——————————>A
     A
     ————————————————<A
           N

The correct prosodic grouping, *un-grammaticality*, follows if the stem is raised to become a functor over the prefix but first backwards-composed with the suffix (Moortgat 1988b: 70; notation translated to result-first):

$$5.5 \quad \begin{array}{ccc} \text{un} & \text{grammatical} & \text{ity} \\ \text{A/A} & \text{A\textbackslash(A/A)} & \text{N\textbackslash A} \end{array}$$

$$\begin{array}{c} \rule{4cm}{0.4pt} \, <\text{C} \\ \text{N\textbackslash(A/A)} \\ \rule{4cm}{0.4pt} \, <\text{A} \\ \text{N} \end{array}$$

Further evidence for the need to have both analyses available comes from the possibility of co-ordination below word level (*zwart- en rood gestreept* ('black- and red stripe + ed'); *peper- en zout kleur ig* ('pepper- and salt colour + ed')) and the classic bracketing ambiguities which result: 'black-and-red-striped ties' or 'black, and red-striped, ties'?

In the case of complement inheritance, however, there are discontinuities involved, and so more power is needed: this is where 'mixed', disharmonic composition is introduced (ibid.: 97; see 1988a: 329; notation again adapted):

$$5.6 \quad \begin{array}{cc} \text{lees} & \text{baar} \\ \text{read} & \text{able} \\ \text{TV} & \text{A\textbackslash TV} \end{array}$$

$$\begin{array}{c} \rule{3cm}{0.4pt} \, <\text{A} \\ \text{A} \end{array}$$

but

$$5.7 \quad \begin{array}{cccc} \text{vergelijk} & \text{baar} & & \text{met} \quad \text{NP} \\ \text{compare} & \text{able} & & \text{with} \quad \text{NP} \\ \text{TV/PP} & \text{A\textbackslash TV} & & \text{PP} \end{array}$$

$$\begin{array}{c} \rule{4cm}{0.4pt} \, \text{Cmixed} \\ \text{A/PP} \\ \rule{5cm}{0.4pt} \, >\text{A} \\ \text{A} \end{array}$$

A 'wrapping' rule which moved the affix into surface position could account for simple cases like this, but would fail on co-ordinated constructions like *his fidelity and devotedness to the king, onvoldaanheid en spijt over de mislukking* ('unhappiness and grief over the failure';

1988a: 332; 1988b: 100), where disharmonic composition and division, suitably restricted entirely by lexical assignment, will still succeed.

The same question is addressed by Hoeksema and Janda (1988), but a rather different answer given.

> The main goal of this paper is to propose an extension of CG in order to enable it to deal with the complexities found in the morphological systems of natural languages. ... Where between the extremes of the Ajdukiewicz/Bar-Hillel systems and the powerful systems envisaged by Curry and Lewis is a theory of CG located which is both adequate and restrictive? In particular, we want to investigate the possibility of keeping the function/argument structure fixed, while extending the operations on expressions.
>
> (1988: 199–200)

In other words, they are trying to do without unary rules like type-raising – exactly those rules for which Moortgat argues – in favour of a wider range of combinatory operations.

The background for this preference is Hockett's (1954) classic distinction between 'Item-and-Arrangement' (IA) and 'Item-and-Process' (IP) in grammatical description. X-bar theory and its derivatives belong to the IA model, concerned mainly with constituency; CGs, with functional categories expressed in terms of input and output (argument and result), are in the expressively richer, derivationally oriented IP model. The description of universal morphology requires a formalization not just of concatenation but of four main (pre-theoretic) types of process: addition, permutation, replacement and subtraction. This extended set of operations is not easily encoded in the slashes of functor categories, so categories are written as triples of argument, output and operation: an English determiner, for example, is ⟨**CN**, **NP**, **Pref**⟩, as it takes a common noun argument, gives a noun phrase result and combines with its argument by prefixation (concatenation to the left).

The range of data discussed in this paper is very wide indeed, drawing on languages of great typological diversity, and giving as full weight to 'exotic' processes like infixation, reduplication and metathesis as to the more familiar forms of simple concatenative affixation and compounding. The analysis of infixation, for example, is particularly interesting. There is extensive evidence – from Latin, Finnish, Warlpiri, Dutch, Chamorro and many other languages –

both of syntactic elements like clitics and of infix morphemes which appear in second or penultimate position in a string. Moortgat (1988b), as we have seen (Ch. 4.ii), introduces the connectives ⟨ and ⟩ to specify these two positions. Hoeksema and Janda (1988: 209) get the same effect by developing Bach's (1984) 'wrapping' rules, RWRAP and LWRAP (see Ch. 4.iii.b above), each with two variants to allow the infixed element to form a grouping with either the preceding or following element(s):

$$\text{RWRAP-pref}(x, y) = (\text{FIRST}(x)(y\ \text{RREST}(x)))$$
$$\text{RWRAP-suff}(x, y) = ((\text{FIRST}(x)y)\text{RREST}(x))$$

$$\text{LWRAP-pref}(x, y) = (\text{LREST}(x)(y\ \text{LAST}(x)))$$
$$\text{LWRAP-suff}(x, y) = ((\text{LREST}(x)y)\text{RREST}(x))$$

This, of course, sacrifices the principle of adjacency, but in a constrained way which the data does seem to demand. The same effect can be achieved through the use of type-raising and -lowering rules – the example is given of Dutch 'verb raising', where the infixation of an auxiliary before the verb cluster can be described either with type-raising (Steedman 1985a) or with wrapping. The main objection made here to raising is that it changes function–argument structure and so the explanatory power of this distinction is lost. Wrapping has no such side-effects, and may be a way of constraining the use of type-changing.

This looks very different from Moortgat's desire to constrain the use of combinatory rules, on the grounds that they are general and so may overgenerate unless arbitrarily restricted. However, Moortgat's infixation connectives in lexically assigned, and restricted, categories correspond exactly to the third member of the triple with which Hoeksema and Janda encode functor categories; wrapping and the other new processes they introduce are general rules in one sense, but will never be used unless called for by a lexically assigned functor category. It is still true, however, that Hoeksema and Janda are much less averse than Moortgat to stipulation of restrictions on rules – 'We are convinced that such limitations indeed exist, but we do not believe that they must be direct consequences of one's descriptive framework' (1988: 241).

The disagreement over the relative merits of type-raising and wrapping is more serious. It is a clear example of the more general debate over unary and binary rules which we have encountered before: is it better to extend the set of two-place operations, so that simple categories can be combined in more different ways, or to extend the set of one-place operations which can coerce categories into the forms they need to combine in simple ways? Binary rules are profligate, and if they overgenerate must be blocked as appropriate by 'opt-out' specifications; unary rules can be viewed as 'opt-in' well-formedness conditions on lexical category assignments; but either, at the end of the day, must be governed by stipulation based on observation of the data. There is no clear 'right answer' on this one – it is a trade-off in which there are arguments on both sides, and in which open-mindedness bids fair to be the most rewarding policy.

5.iii SYNTAX

The greatest part of categorial linguistic description has looked at syntactic phenomena, either assuming or to some degree developing an integral compositional semantics for any syntactic derivation. The provisos at the beginning of this chapter are thus most strongly applicable here: it has only been possible to give a very partial account of the current body of work, based on the more easily available primary sources, and even at that it will be largely an account of inter-denominational squabbles within a very broad church. CGs are badly in need of a bit more standardization, and of more work which builds on previous proposals rather than replying with yet more counter-proposals. Diversity is healthy, but miscellaneity is not.

The other pattern which emerges when one tries to compile a representative sample of CG syntactic work is the patchiness of its linguistic coverage. Some constructions, like co-ordination and unbounded dependency, have been intensely debated; others, like the internal structure of noun phrases, have been largely ignored, perhaps because they seemed likely to shed less light on the fundamental concern of how far to push the limits of the formalism.

More serious than the neglect of various specific constructions, however, is the general neglect of the relations between constructions. Much of the motivation for the first transformational grammars lay in the desire to capture the regular relations between active and passive sentences, the two English ditransitive constructions and so on. Early moves towards lexicalism had the same focus. The other major unification-based grammars have well-developed rule types for these regularities, such as the 'meta-rules' of Generalized Phrase Structure Grammar and the 'lexical rules' of Lexical-Functional Grammar. Montague Grammar, explicitly replying to the challenge of the then dominant transformational paradigm, did address the issue – see especially Partee (1976) and Davis and Mithun (1979) for the best collections of work in this vein, and Dowty (1979a) for a similar proposal informed by Generative Semantics, and for the first time recognizably lexicalist. But more recent CGs have said far too little about it, and will not be able to produce a complete and comprehensive account of language until they say more.

5.iii.a Passives

As just mentioned, it seems to have become traditional for the passive construction to be among the first described by any new linguistic theory. In Chomsky (1957) it is one of three constructions (together with conjunction and auxiliary-verb clusters) which dispute the adequacy of previous conceptions of phrase structure, and show the need for transformational rules (1957: 42–3, 77–81). The primary source *par excellence* for LFG, Bresnan (1982), opens with Bresnan's paper on 'The passive in lexical theory', and with the claim that 'passivization is so inextricably connected to the central grammatical systems of complementation in many languages that it poses major challenges for any lexical analysis' (ibid.: 3); she cites almost a dozen references from the early 1970s onwards which use passive as a central test case in exploring the viability of lexicalist syntactic analysis. It is one of the first meta-rules introduced in Gazdar's (1982) early programmatic statement 'Phrase Structure Grammar', and in the GPSG book (Gazdar *et al.* 1985); and so on. This has not happened by chance or by arcane arbitrary convention: passive is typologically widespread, and is a paradigm case of two central natural language phenomena for which any linguistic theory must have some good explanation, the sharing of a common 'meaning' by different surface forms and the ability of verbs (or indeed any functors) to appear in a systematically related range of different valency, or subcategorization, patterns.

The early CG accounts of passive are explicit responses to transformational accounts, and do not always appear dramatically different, except in their integration of semantics with syntax. Partee's (1973) 'Some transformational extensions of Montague Grammar' includes rules for reflexivization, tough movement, subject-raising and object-raising as well as passivization and passive agent deletion, 'in essentially their classical forms' (ibid.: 65), but with the corresponding explicitly formalized semantic translation rule given as part of each: thus (I have given an interlinear gloss, in round brackets, for the first rule, which should make the second clear also):

2.3.2 *Passive.* If $\phi \in P_t$ and ϕ has the form:
(If a given sentence ϕ is a member of the set P of phrases of category **t** (sentence), of the form:)

(a) *strict form:* $_t[_T[\alpha]_{IV}[_{TV}[\beta]_T[him_i]\gamma]]$

(a **t** (sentence), made up of a **T** (term-phrase) $[\alpha]$, followed by an **IV** (verb phrase, or intransitive verb) which is itself made up of a **TV** (transitive verb) $[\beta]$ followed by the **T** $[him_i]$ and maybe some other stuff (γ))

(b) *loose form:* $_t[_T[\alpha]_{IV}[_{TV}[\beta]_T[\delta]\gamma]]$

(the same, but with the variable δ, for any direct object)

then $F_{101}(\phi) \in P_t$, where $F_{101}(\phi)$ is:

(then the result of applying the rule F_{101} to the sentence ϕ is also a member of the set of sentences:)

$$_t\left[_T\left[\begin{Bmatrix} \text{(a)} & he_i \\ \text{(b)} & \delta \end{Bmatrix}\right]_{IV}[is\ EN_{TV}[\beta]\gamma[by_T[\alpha]]]\right]$$

(a **t** (sentence), made up of a **T** (term-phrase) $[he_i]$ in the specific case (a) or δ in the general case (b), followed by an **IV** (verb phrase, or intransitive verb) which is itself made up of the **EN** form (passive participle) of the **TV** (transitive verb) $[\beta]$, followed by whatever other stuff was there before (γ), followed by *by* and the **T** $[\alpha]$)

> *Example:* John sees him₂ → he₂ is seen by John.
> *Translation rule:* identity mapping.

2.3.3 *Passive agent deletion.* If $\phi \in P_t$ and ϕ has the form:

$$_t[_T[he_i]_{IV}[is\ EN_{TV}[\beta][by\ him_j]]]$$

then $F_{102}(\phi) \in P_t$, where $F_{102}(\phi)$ is:

$$_t[_T[he_i]_{IV}[is\ EN_{TV}[\beta]]]$$

Example: he_1 is loved by $him_3 \rightarrow he_1$ is loved.
Translation rule: If $\phi \in P_t$ and ϕ translates into ϕ',
then $F_{102}(\phi)$ translates into $(\exists x_j)\phi'$.

(ibid.: 66)

The semantic foundation of Montague Grammar is evident not only in the care taken over the semantic formulation of these rules, but also in the overall focus of Partee's concern: the agentless passive 'is expressed as a rule which syntactically deletes a free variable but semantically adds an existential quantifier over that variable' (ibid.: 65), and the discussion which follows turns mainly on the problems of quantifier scope assignment in the derived constructions.

Another of the classic Montague Grammar papers is Bach's (1980) 'In Defense of Passive'. Bach argues (as does Keenan 1980) that passive is defined on a phrasal category **T**(ransitive)**V**(erb)**P**(hrase) – 'a phrase which works syntactically and semantically like a transitive verb, and not a verb phrase that contains a transitive verb' (Bach 1980: 299) – not on sentences. The possibility of passivization is a diagnostic for whether a verb phrase is really transitive: the acceptability of *John was persuaded to go* shows that *persuade to go* is transitive, the unacceptability of **John was promised to go* shows that *promise to go* is not. This is reflected in their (directionally neutral) category assignments. *Persuade* has the category **TVP|IVP**, a function from an intransitive verb phrase such as *to go* to a **TVP**. *Promise* takes an **NP** (*John*) to form a function from an **IVP** (*to go*) to another **IVP** (*promise John to go*); thus the category **(IVP|IVP)|NP** (ibid.: 300).

Again, semantic criteria are essential in the exploration that follows. Bach concludes that

There is a syntactic category of Passive verb phrases (**PVP**) which can be combined with *be* to form an **IVP**, but can occur independently as well. Semantically, **PVP**'s are taken to be predicatives, that is, expressions of some category $t/^n e$, denoting sets of entities (e.g. individual concepts). The rules are these:

Agentless Passive Verb Phrases (**PVP**):
If $\gamma \in$ **TVP**, then $EN(\gamma) \in$ **PVP**, where $EN(\gamma)$ is the result of making (or choosing) the past participle form of the main verb(s) in γ.

Translation rule: if γ translates as γ', then $EN(\gamma)$ translates as $\lambda x \exists y [\gamma'(^\wedge\lambda P \; P(x))] \, (y)$

Agentive **PVP**:

If $\alpha \in$ **NP** and $\gamma \in$ **TVP**, then $EN(\gamma)$ *by* $\alpha \in$ **PVP**

Translation rule: if α translates as α' and γ as γ', then $EN(\gamma)$ *by* α translates as $\lambda x \alpha'(y(\gamma'(^\wedge\lambda P \; P(x)))(y))$

Simplified translations for two examples would be these:

> (John was) *injured*: $\lambda x \exists y [\text{injure}'(y, x)]$
> (John was) *seen by Mary*: $\lambda x [\text{see}'(m, x)]$

Thus *John was injured* is interpreted as meaning that John was such that someone injured him; *John was seen by Mary* is interpreted as saying that John was such that Mary saw him. ... I assume that *be* and *get*, at least, are assigned to a category **IVP/PVP**.

> (ibid.: 314–15)

Bach offers extended arguments, from a wide range of English data, to support the validity of **PVP** as a distinct syntactic category, and for the claim that passive is phrasal rather than lexical. From this follows the need for **TVP** as a category for passivization to apply to. But no such category can exist in a transformationally-based phrase-structure account, as they can look only at the set of possible phrase-structure environments for a verb, and these may be the same for verbs whose transitivity differs, such as *strike* and *regard*. So the argument – much of which is careful to be largely theory-neutral – does turn out to favour CGs:

> If the analysis proposed here is correct, then it follows that the general framework of CG is to be preferred over other frameworks which leave no room for such a category.

> (ibid.: 320)

Bach's position is taken in contrast both to transformational linguistics and to the then fledgling lexicalist grammars. But early lexical grammar had its categorial incarnation too, most notably in the work of David Dowty (1978, 1979a, 1982). I have mentioned before (Ch. 2.iv) the blend of Generative Semantics and Montague Grammar with which Dowty (1979a) re-interprets the principal classic governed transformations of Chomskyan Standard Theory as lexical rules in a CG. Further challenged by the emergence of Relational Grammar, Dowty (1982) proposes a universal characterization of grammatical relations according to the argument structure of functor categories. Functors apply to exactly one argument at a time, the 'single argument' principle:

> A verb that ultimately takes *n* arguments is always treated as combining by a syntactic rule with exactly one argument to produce a phrase of the same category as a verb of $n - 1$ arguments.
>
> (1982: 84)

Rules are expressed as ordered triples of ⟨syntactic operation, input sequence of categories, output category⟩: for example, an intransitive verb (predicate, **IV**) and a term phrase (subject, **T**) together form a truth-value-bearing expression (sentence, **t**), a transitive verb and a term phrase form a predicate:

> S1: ⟨F₁,⟨IV,T⟩,t⟩ (Subject–Predicate Rule)
> S2: ⟨F₂,⟨TV,T⟩,IV⟩ (Verb–Direct Object Rule)
>
> (ibid.: 85)

The syntactic operations used will differ widely between languages – an impressive range of cross-linguistic data illustrate this – but

> we will define any term phrase in any language that is combined with an **IV** via S1 as a subject term, and any term phrase that is combined with a **TV** via S2 as a direct object; moreover, these are language independent semantic definitions as well, since the semantic rules corresponding to S1 and S2 will be the same in each language.
>
> (ibid.: 87)

Rules which affect grammatical relations – by reducing or extending the number of arguments a verb takes, or re-arranging them – do so by changing the category of the functor, also according to universal patterns (see Ch. 6.iii below). The agentless passive is a relation-reducing rule:

S6: $\langle F_6, \langle TV \rangle, IV \rangle$ (Agentless Passive)
Semantic Operation: $\lambda y(\exists x)[(\alpha'(y))(x)]$
English: $F_6(\alpha) = be^\wedge \alpha'$, where α' is the passive form of α.

(ibid.: 92)

Agentive or 'full' passive is a relation-rearranging rule:

S7: $\langle F_7, \langle TV, T \rangle, IV \rangle$ (Agentive Passive)
Semantic Operation: $\lambda x[(\alpha'(x))(\beta')]$
English: $F_7(\alpha, \beta) = be^\wedge \alpha'^\wedge by^\wedge \beta'$, where α' is the passive form of α and β' is the accusative form of β.

(ibid.)

(although Dowty suggests later that the agent in full passives is really instrumental, ibid.: 117–18).

Extended arguments are given for preferring this approach to that of either transformational grammar (TG) or Relational Grammar: universals of word order, and the treatment of discontinuous constituents, favour this definition of grammatical relations. The description of relation-changing rules as rules changing the category of verbs is supported by evidence from 'structure-preserving' rules, from the fact that 'relation-changing' morphology (like passivization) is marked on verbs, and that the rules are lexically governed by verbs.

Dowty makes it clear, however, that this is not the all-out lexicalism of Bresnan's position. Category-changing rules can be either lexical or syntactic. In particular, the passivization rule must be syntactic, as it can apply to syntactically complex units (whole phrases, derived **TV**s, Bach's **TVP**s) as well as to lexical **TV**s. Two types of data illustrate this: verb–complement clusters can be passivized:

John gave Mary a book / Mary was given a book by John
Mary appointed John chairman / John was appointed chairman by
  Mary

as can verb–purpose clause groups, where the purpose clause is argued (after Bach 1982) to modify the **TV** and thus to be part of the passivized **TVP**:

> The truck was bought (for Bill) to deliver groceries in.
>
> (ibid.: 102)

Further arguments in favour of this categorial account of grammatical relations and relation-changing rules are based on complementation, causativization, and wanna-contraction. The final argument is one characteristically claimed for CGs, that of theoretical simplicity: here, specifically,

> the theory of RG is presently stated as a large body of axioms, or laws, most of which are entirely independent of one another. ... what I have proposed all results from Montague's general approach to syntax and semantics, plus only two principles: the 'single argument' principle ... and the assumption that relation-changing rules are operations on verbs, not on full sentences. All the rest follows as a consequence of these assumptions.
>
> (ibid.: 107)

Dowty is quick to admit, however, that there is syntactic counter-evidence to his proposals, especially from ergative languages, and from the unclarity of the distinction (crucial to his account) between arguments and modifiers. (For example, the agent phrase in a full passive looks very much like an instrumental modifier.) He admits freely, too, that his proposal is much less detailed than those he is arguing against. I think it is fair to say that this marks much good work in the CG paradigm: an entirely appropriate concern with underlying principles and with the properties of the general framework is often addressed at the cost of really extensive and detailed specific linguistic analyses such as some other, perhaps more narrowly dogmatic, theories are producing.

That is certainly true of Keenan and Timberlake's (1988) paper 'Extending categorial grammar', which, like Dowty's, develops a foundational, language-universal proposal, well motivated by a wide range of cross-linguistic data, but short on detailed syntactic analyses. They propose '*n*-tuple' categories to capture the generalizations across different valency frames for the 'same' functor: for example, the English verb *be* can act as **VP/AP** (*John is angry*) or as **VP/NP** (*John is a winner*), and so has the *n*-tuple category ⟨**VP,VP**⟩/ ⟨**AP,NP**⟩ (1988: 266). Valency-changing rules are themselves defined as functor categories from one tuple to another. Passivization takes a functor over n arguments to a functor over $n - 1$ arguments. English applies this to transitive verbs – in Keenan and Timberlake's notation, P_2 to P_1 – and to ditransitives (P_3 to P_2). Lithuanian allows P_1 to P_0 – thus the delightfully glossed

> Ar buta tenai langiniu?
> been there windows
> 'And had there really been any existing going on by windows there?'

(ibid.: 275)

and in Kinyarwanda 'Passive can "promote" ... any of the three object arguments of a P_4' (ibid.), thus P_4 to P_3. The universal statement of the passivization rule is thus

(a)
$$\dfrac{S}{A_nA_1...A_{n-1}} \Bigg/ \dfrac{S}{AA_1...A_n} \qquad n \in \{0, 1, 2, 3\}$$

(b) $\text{pass}(p_{n+1})(x_{n-1})...(x_1)(x_n) = (\exists y)(p_{n+1})(x_n)...(x_1)(y)$

(ibid.: 276)

No further gloss or detail is given – understandably, as the authors are painting a large picture with quick broad brush-strokes, of which this is only one. But that emphasis is symptomatic of much recent work in/on CGs; and, while it should not be discouraged, it should certainly be supplemented by more substantial linguistic description.

CG accounts of passive thus offer a good illustration of how the field has developed, and of how it now stands: from an acceptance of many aspects of the transformational paradigm, but with careful formalization of an integral compositional semantics inspired by Montague, in the early 1970s, through an increasingly critical response to the growing diversity of linguistic theories that followed, to a fully independent major paradigm, rightly working to articulate its fundamental principles and basic mechanisms, rightly concerned to find language-universal principles from which language-specific grammars follow naturally, but often thereby leaving itself too little time to develop those grammars for more than disjoint fragments of a few languages.

5.iii.b 'Raising' and 'control'

The inverse of the passive problem for transformational grammar was presented by sets of sentences such as

5.8 (a) Chris promised Sandy to leave.
5.9 (a) Chris persuaded Sandy to leave.
5.10 (a) Chris believed Tigger to be hungry.
5.11 (a) Chris wanted Sandy to feed Tigger.

Rather than one 'deep structure' underlying two different 'surface structures', here the same surface structure could be the realization of quite different deep structures:

5.8 (b) Chris promised Sandy (Chris to leave)
5.9 (b) Chris persuaded Sandy (Sandy to leave)
5.10 (b) Chris believed (Tigger be hungry)
5.11 (b) Chris wanted (Sandy feed Tigger)

All four sentences take the surface form of a main verb with an infinitival complement, but the semantic relations between the main verbs and the arguments within their complements are dramatically different. In 5.8, the subject of the main verb is also the understood subject of the infinitive, and was said to have been present in both clauses at deep-structure level and removed from the embedded clause by 'Equi NP Deletion'. In 5.10, the subject of the embedded clause was said to have been 'raised' to the position (*sic*) of object in the main clause (see Postal 1974 for great detail), while in 5.9 and 5.11, the object of the main clause 'controlled' the embedded subject position, that is, determined its referential properties, including agreement. These distinctions were reinforced by systematic differences in the range of syntactic behaviour which these classes of verbs allowed. In particular, verbs like *promise* cannot appear in the passive: **Sandy was promised to leave.* Jackendoff (1972: esp. Ch. 5) is early in using such data as evidence for underlying 'thematic relations' which are expressed in deep structure; in Williams (1980, with comprehensive earlier references) they depend on 'predicate structure', in an early Government–Binding framework.

The history of CG's dealings with 'raising' and 'control' is similar to that for passive (not surprisingly, given how closely the two were linked in transformational theory): early meticulous attempts, mainly by Emmon Bach, to adapt a Chomskyan analysis to a Montague framework, nascent lexicalism from David Dowty, and then little but passing mentions intended to support wide programmatic statements, until Jacobson's intelligently eclectic (1990) 'Raising as function composition'.

McCawley (1979) looks at 'some transformational analyses that could in an interesting way be reworked into Montague analyses', but in a very conservative way – typically,

> An analysis with Raising for sentences like *Most of the students seem to have failed the exam* has strong semantic points in its favor in that it readily yields a semantic interpretation in which *seem* has higher scope than *most*, i.e., an interpretation paraphrasable as 'It seems as if most of the students have failed the exam'. Without 'Most of the students failed the exam' as a syntactic constituent, it is hard to see how the semantics could be compositional.
>
> (1979: 114)

(Oehrle has pointed out to me (p.c.) that

> There is a compositional lexical entry for *seem* which easily overcomes the difficulty [Lambek format]:
>
> **seem**: $(np \backslash s)/inf$: $\lambda f \cdot \lambda Q \cdot \mathbf{seem}'(Qf)$
>
> According to this entry, there is no syntactic constituent which corresponds to *Most of the students failed the exam*, but application of the interpretation of *seem* to its arguments and two rounds of β-reduction yield a semantic constituent corresponding to 'Most of the students failed the exam'.

This solution, by accepting a mismatch between syntax and semantics, would not be appealing to a categorial purist, but it is not out of character with the slightly wider perspective of type theory.)

Given the insistent connection between raising and passive, it is not surprising to find that both Bach's (1979b) 'Control in Montague Grammar' and his (1980) 'In defense of passive' relate the two phenomena. The second paper, developing ideas suggested in the first, opens with the *promise/persuade* problem. Bach's answer, as we have seen (Ch.5.iii.a), is to assign different (directionally neutral) categories to *promise* **(IVP|IVP)|NP** and *persuade* **TVP|IVP**. As all and only transitive verb phrases can occur in the passive, *persuade* together with its complement is correctly predicted to passivize, while *promise* at no point forms (part of) a **TVP** and so cannot. Dowty (1982: 103–5) elaborates on this category assignment:

> Bach suggests that it is a systematic principle that when an infinitive complement of a verb is syntactically controlled by an **NP** outside the infinitive – i.e. when this **NP** triggers reflexive agreement or number agreement within the infinitive – and when this **NP** is involved in semantic entailments with respect to the infinitive, then this **NP** must be the next higher argument of the verb after the infinitive.

In *Chris persuaded Michael to feed himself* the infinitive is controlled by *Michael*, which is both the understood subject and the trigger for reflexivization, so the structure is something like ((*persuade to feed himself*) *Michael*) *Chris*. In *Chris promised Michael to leave*, it is the matrix subject **NP** *Chris* which is the controller and understood subject of *to leave*, so the structure must be ((*promise Michael*) *to leave*) *Chris*. The structure of the functor categories follows from their semantics: *persuade* combines first with the intransitive infinitive and then with its object, thus **TVP|IVP**, while *promise* combines most closely with its object, then with the infinitive **IVP**, and after that with the subject, thus **(IVP|IVP)|NP**.

The question of control in purpose clauses is addressed in Bach (1982). In a purpose clause with two 'gaps', like *I bought 'War and Peace' to read to the children* (1982: 35), the object of *read* is clearly controlled by, that is, co-referential with, the object of *bought*. The intended subject of the embedded verb is less obvious. It could be the subject of the main verb, but need not be: compare *I bought 'Bambi' to give to Mary to pass on to John to take along on the camping trip to read to the children* (ibid.: 54), where the most likely controller for the subject of *read* is *John*, because it is John who ends up in physical possession of the book. Thus, while Bach proposes a careful non-transformational context-free phrase-structure grammar for purpose clauses, of a type similar to work by Dowty, Gazdar and others at the time, complete with a Montague semantics, he concludes that discourse factors and simple common sense may be more important in the end. (A similarly pragmatic approach is taken by Laduslaw and Dowty 1988.)

Meanwhile, more radically, following his (1978) general programme of 'Governed transformations as lexical rules in a Montague Grammar', Dowty (1979b) had proposed a non-transformational analysis of raising in particular, and had no doubt of its significance:

> Thomason's (1976) non-transformational method of dealing with passive sentences can be extended to cases related by the transformations Raising to Subject and Raising to Object. That is, a 'raised' sentence such as *A Republican seems certain to win* would not be derived transformationally from *It seems that it is certain that a Republican will win*, but would rather be produced independently and related to this second sentence only by semantic rules. The same comment applies to *A unicorn is believed by Bill to be expected by John to be found by Mary* and *Bill believes that John expects Mary to find a unicorn*, where both Passive and Raising (to Object) are involved in the usual transformational analysis. Since the Passive and Raising transformations are crucially involved in arguments about some very basic assumptions about transformational theory (e.g., the transformational cycle), a theory of syntax which could get along without these transformations might be strikingly different from the familiar transformational one.
>
> (1979b: 155)

'Dative movement', the principal object of Dowty's concern in this paper, is argued in considerable formal detail to be best expressed as a category-changing rule, in effect a word-formation rule – a special case of the general argument of Dowty (1979a).

> Finally, category-changing lexical rules as described in this paper can be used to account for the different homophonous basic expressions Thomason is forced to postulate in his treatment of verb complements and Raising sentences. That is, Thomason treats *expect* as a basic expression in three different syntactic categories in order to produce examples like (64):

(64) a. John expected that Mary would leave.
     b. John expected Mary to leave.
     c. John expected to leave.

But we can instead take *expect* in one of these categories as basic and write lexical rules accounting for the change in grammatical category and for the appropriate meaning of the other two verbs in terms of the first. As was the case with the rules discussed in this paper, there are lexical exceptions to the Raising rules, and cases can be found where Raising introduces a subtle unpredict-able change in meaning (see Postal 1974). Thus the same sort of motivation is present for treating the Raising rules as lexical rules as that observed for Dative and Object Deletion.

Indeed, it now seems reasonable to me to hypothesize that *all* cases of lexically governed transformations and/or transforma-tions that 'change meaning' can and should be treated as lexical rules along the lines laid out in this paper.

(ibid.: 212–13; Dowty 1979a: 307 quoted in Ch.2.iv above)

Since then, control phenomena have been mentioned, in passing, in a number of frameworks, including Combinatory CG (e.g. Steedman 1988: 429), Unification CG (e.g. Zeevat *et al.* 1987: 209–11), and Klein and Sag's (1985) 'type-driven translation'. One of the more unusual is Keenan and Timberlake's (1988) proposal to extend CG with '*n*-tuple categories', outlined above (Ch.5.iii.a). The encoding of alternative patterns in a single category means that words with par-tially overlapping behaviour can be assigned partially overlapping categories. *Promise/persuade* offers a prime example of partial overlap, as they can take superficially identical infinitival comple-ments, but diverge both in their other syntactic possibilities and in their semantic interpretation (ibid.: 287ff.). And an interesting hybrid is Chierchia's (1988: 144–6) view of control as a form of predication, to be formalized, on a base of essentially normal CG complex categories, in something like the Control Agreement Principle of GPSG. An indexing mechanism on the arguments in complex categories ensures the correct co-reference, and thus the correct agreement properties:

try: $(S/NP_n)/IV_n$
force: $((S/NP)/NP_n)/IV_n$
promise: $((S/NP_n)/IV)/NP_n$

This is argued to retain the baby, but not the bathwater, of Chomskyan Standard Theory within a categorial system.

There is one careful and thorough recent categorial discussion of raising, Jacobson's (1990) 'Raising as function composition'. 'Equi' verbs like *try* have classically been taken to denote a relation between individuals and propositions, so that in *John tries to be nice* the embedded VP *tries to be nice* must at some level of representation be an S, with a specified subject *John* which does not appear on the sur-face. Recent work by Dowty (1978, 1985) and Chierchia proposes instead that *try* denotes a relation between an individual and a property, not a proposition, so that the fact that *John* is the 'understood subject' of *to be nice* is a consequence of the lexical entailments associated with *try*. Jacobson refers to this as the 'lexical entailment theory of Equi', or 'LE Equi', and agrees with it. The analogous theory of 'LE Raising', however, put forward in the same sources – the view that '*seem* is just like *try* both in its syntax and in its semantic type: it too denotes a relation between an individual and a property, and here too control is a matter of lexical entailments' (1990: 425) – she argues against, from a range of systematic syntactic differences between Equi and raising constructions.

Jacobson agrees with the traditional view of raising, against LE Raising, that *seem* denotes a one-place relation which takes a proposition as argument, and selects only for an S complement. Like LE Raising, however, she rejects the traditional claims that at some level of representation the embedded VP in [*John seems to be nice*] has a subject, and that this subject 'raises', by a movement rule, to become the matrix subject. She accepts, therefore, that there is a mismatch here between syntax and semantics. The solution to this mismatch is a highly restricted use of function composition ('FC Raising'):

> it is only under this view that one can provide a natural account of why an item which subcategorizes for an S complement actually combines with a VP complement to give rise to the Raising construction.
>
> (ibid.: 427)

A Raising to Subject verb like *seem* has the category S/S, giving such derivations as:

5.12　seem　　°　　to be tall
　　　　S/S　　　　　　S/NP
　　　　————————————————
　　　　　　seem to be tall
　　　　　　　　S/NP
　　　　　　　　　　　seem$'$ ° be-tall$'$ = $\lambda P[\text{seem}'(\text{be-tall}'(P))]$

　　　　　　　　　　　　　　　　　　　　(ibid.: 431)

'A Raising to Object verb like *expect* is of category **(S/NP)/S**. When it function composes with an **S/NP** like *to be nice* the result is the **(S/NP)/NP** (i.e., the transitive verb) *expect to be nice*. This then takes as argument an object to give a **VP** such as *expect John to be nice*' (ibid.: 432). (Note that the slash connectives are non-directional, that the object is the last element to be composed into the **VP**, and that this requires the use of wrapping.) The fact that any category restrictions imposed by the embedded **VP** on its subject are 'inherited' by the 'raised' constituent, commonly used as an argument in favour of a movement analysis, follows from the nature of function composition:

> If the embedded **VP** requires some constituent of category **X** in subject position then − by definition − it is a functor of category **S/X**. When it function composes with a Raising verb such as *seem* of category **S/S** the composed function will (by the definition of function composition) be of category **S/X**.
>
> (ibid.: 429)

The use of composition is restricted, though, to lexical functors explicitly licensed for it, by the introduction of a 'composition' slash connective $^*/$. Thus the category of a Raising to Subject verb like *seem* or *tend* is S^*/S, a Raising to Subject adjective is A^*/S, and a Raising to Object verb is an $(S/NP)^*/S$. Functors with the traditional simple slash connective can apply only by function application. This prevents overgeneration and the 'spurious ambiguity' problem associated with the wholesale use of function composition. Division rules (see Ch. 3.v) have been used to achieve the same effect, of using a lexically licensed, so in some sense naturally constrained, category where its power is needed, rather than a general rule of function composition extrinsically constrained to avoid overgeneration. Jacobson's composition connective is simpler, clearer and does not add recursive power to the grammar.

The most significant broader implication of this account is that, contrary to the claims of 'radical lexicalism', not everything can happen in the lexicon: 'there is a real division of labour between lexical and syntactic processes' (ibid.: 428). A number of properties, such as case and number agreement, are shown to hold of categories which are derived by composition, and so cannot be lexically assigned. This is very similar to Dowty's argument that passive is syntactic, not lexical, as it too applies to elements which do not exist in the lexicon but are derived syntactically.

Apart from Jacobson's well-argued proposal, however, raising and control offer another example of problems whose solution is recognized to be essential for a complete grammar, but which, once CG had outgrown its early reactionary phase, have not quite seemed exciting enough to attract the necessary degree of attention from ordinary working categorial grammarians. Sooner or later this area will have to be back-filled, as it were, behind the more exotic problems which have seemed more attractive, and to which we turn next.

5.iii.c Curious dependencies: unbounded, discontinuous, multiple and crossing

If early TG found in passives and control relations evidence that the deep-to-surface mapping was unique in neither direction, more serious problems were posed by constructions in which surface elements appeared in an order which disrupted the presumed underlying constituent structure. Classic examples of 'discontinuous constituency', or 'discontinuous dependency', are the 'fronting' of objects, as in *who did you see?*, and the separation of verbs from their particles, as in *he looked it up*. The solution adopted in TG was to posit movement rules which applied to deep structures like *you did see who*, *he looked up it* and produced the desired surface output – Paul Postal's (1974) *On Raising* is a particularly thorough early exploration of this approach.

A classical CG offered no obvious way to deal with discontinuous dependency, and indeed, as we have seen (Ch.2.iii.b), it was this class of problems which led Bar-Hillel to abandon the enterprise in the early 1960s. Its importance has remained obvious, and two approaches have been developed, one based on extending the rule system while preserving adjacency, the other keeping a simpler binary and unary rule set but adding wrapping operations, abandoning adjacency – exactly the alternatives (not surprisingly) that we have already seen developed to describe bracketing paradoxes and infixation in morphology (Ch.5.ii). An early, clear example of the former is the treatment of 'unbounded dependency' in Ades and Steedman (1982), which I will describe first. I will then look at the debate over a wider range of raising and extraction constructions, concluding with a briefer discussion of multiple dependencies (parasitic gaps) and crossing dependencies.

'Unbounded' dependency is so called because the 'raised' object at the beginning of the sentence can belong in a sentential complement embedded arbitrarily deep: *Who did you see?*, *Who does she think you saw?*, *Who did Chris say Pat thought you saw?* and so on. Any natural way to describe this will be recursive: the 'raising' transformation was cyclic, 'lifting' the object out of one embedded clause after another. Ades and Steedman use the recursive power of generalized composition to build onwards from the main clause until a 'derivational constituent' is formed which can apply (backwards) to the fronted object and give the correct semantic interpretation:

5.13 Who(m)   do you think   he loves?
　　　NP　　　　　S|S　　　　S|NP
　　　　　　　　　　————————————>C
　　　　　　　　　　　　S|NP
　　————————————————————————<A
　　　　　　　　S

5.14 Who   do you think　　loves　　him?
　　　NP　　　S|S　　S|NP|NP　　NP
　　　　　　　————————————>C
　　　　　　　　　S|NP|NP
　　————————————————————<A
　　　　　　S|NP
　　————————————————————————>A
　　　　　　　　　S

(1982: 546)

(Notice, as above (Ch. 4.iii.a), that in this account, unlike most, the object argument is consistently incorporated after the subject.) Superficially similar examples like *This man I burned a book about* or *This man I met a girl who knew* are correctly predicted to be ungrammatical because (for independent reasons) composition into NP is not allowed. 'Extraction is possible if and only if a structure can be "penetrated" by Partial Combination [composition]' (ibid.: 549), which is not true of the NPs *a book about this man* or *a girl who met this man*. This one basic constraint does the work of a number of 'negative' rules in TG, such as the Left Branch Condition and many constraints on Root constructions.

The insights and motivations here are in many ways similar to those of Gazdar's work of about the same time. In general terms, Steedman and Gazdar were both looking for a simpler grammar formalism than the by then highly complex, not to say convoluted, mathematically intractable and formally undecidable state of transformational grammar. Surface constraints should follow from properly motivated underlying principles, the formal and computational properties of the grammar should be well understood, and semantics (Montague-based) should have an integral place in a principled relation to syntax.

Categories are not (all) atomic objects, but can be complex symbols with a rich information content.

In particular, they both connected the non-standard structures 'left' by 'extraction' with those found in 'non-constituent' co-ordination. The connection is worked out in detail in Gazdar's (1981) 'Unbounded dependencies and coordinate structure' and Steedman's (1985a) 'Dependency and coordination in the grammar of Dutch and English'. Co-ordination will be discussed shortly (Ch.5.iii.d). Steedman's (1985a) basic account of extraction in English develops his earlier proposal slightly, clarifying the step from simple to generalized composition, and using type-raising as an alternative to backward combination rules. This gives derivations like 5.15, where the fronted topic NP has been raised to the (non-directional) category of a function into a topicalized sentence from a function-into-a-sentence-from-an-NP, that is, a subject and transitive verb together looking for their object; recall that the $ notation stands for the remainder, if any, carried forward by generalized composition:

5.15

Those cakes	I	can	believe	that	she	will	eat
T$\|(S$|NP)	S|FVP	FVP|VP	VP|S'	S'|S	S|FVP	FVP|VP	VP|NP

```
                 ─────────────>C
                     S|VP
                 ─────────────────────>C
                             S|S'
                                 ──────────────>C
                                     S|S
                                         ──────────────>C
                                             S|FVP
                                                 ──────────────>C
                                                     S|VP
                                                         ──────────────>C
                                                             S|NP
─────────────────────────────────────────────────────────────────────>A
                 T
```

(1985a: 535)

Gazdar is concerned to show that unbounded dependencies, despite their open-ended nature, are within the descriptive power of a phrase-structure grammar. The fact that syntactic categories in GPSG are complex symbols allows him to introduce a distinction between 'basic' and 'derived' categories. Basic categories are a specified finite set V_N. The set $D(V_N)$ of derived categories is defined as $D(V_N) = \{\alpha/\beta : \alpha, \beta V_N\}$, where 'intuitively ... α/β labels a node of type

α which dominates material containing a hole of type β (i.e. an extraction site on a movement analysis). So, for example, S/NP is a sentence which has an NP missing somewhere' (Gazdar 1982: 168). A parallel set of derived rules is also needed, which allow these derived categories to enter into otherwise normal syntactic structures: these rules must each expand a derived category in such a way that its 'hole' is also found in its expansion, so that information about 'missing' items can be carried up and down the tree. Gazdar can then produce derivations like:

5.16 To Sandy Kim wants to give Fido

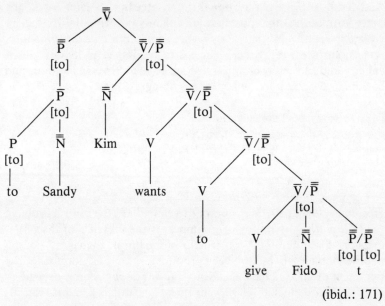

(ibid.: 171)

This 'slash' notation for extraction looks misleadingly similar to the CG slash connective, especially here: it is important to understand the difference. The GPSG slash is defined on the base of a set of phrase-structure rules, and indicates a constituency relation; the CG slash indicates a functional relation, in a system which rejects phrase-structure rules and conventional constituency relations. A slashed category in GPSG is an augmentation for special cases, in CG the basic device for expressing normal function/argument relations. As a reflex of this contrast, GPSG derived categories require a special set of derived rules, while CG complex categories use the normal combination rules. As a particularly striking illustration of the difference (which I owe to Pete Whitelock), think of the category NP/NP: in CG it denotes a function from a nominal to a nominal, that is, an adjective, and in GPSG a nominal missing a nominal, in other words a trace.

Although thus far I find Steedman's account of unbounded dependency more natural, economical and elegant than Gazdar's, it has serious problems of its own. The most significant of these is probably the largely unwelcome context-sensitive power of generalized composition. The constraint against composition into nominal categories may also look uncomfortably *ad hoc*, although less so than the assortment of constraints on transformations which it replaces. And if categories are directional, as in Steedman's later work, the exact form of the topic-raising rule is slightly problematic. It needs to violate the constraint that raising rules should preserve directionality, that is, surface word order, it needs to be limited in its domain of validity and to sentence-initial position to avoid overgeneration, and Steedman describes its semantics as 'obscure': thus

> Topicalization
> $\#X \Rightarrow \#St/(S/X)$
> where $X \in \{NP, PP, VP, AP, S'\}$

> (1987: 414)

The importance of the problem is generally recognized – indeed, Steedman (1988: 420) goes so far as to claim that 'the central problem for CG, as for any theory of grammar, is the presence of discontiguous or "discontinuous" constructions in natural languages' – and a number of alternatives have been proposed within CG, not just for the treatment of unbounded dependency but for discontinuous dependencies in general, including wh-movement and topicalization, various forms of raising, parasitic gaps and verb gapping and so on. The debate, as noted before, is principally between the use of sometimes over-powerful unary rules and generalizations of function composition, respecting adjacency (as in Steedman's proposals discussed above), and of surface wrapping or scrambling rules which keep to a simpler underlying calculus but give up the Adjacency Hypothesis. The first approach is further represented by Moortgat (1988a, 1988b), with a cautionary reservation in Dowty (1988). Syntactic wrapping rules are preferred by Chierchia (1988), and Pareschi (1988) also gives up adjacency. Both Huck (1988) and Pollard (1988) strike an eclectic balance, finding a place for both, as we shall see.

Moortgat (1988a) handles 'a number of discontinuous dependencies and bracketing paradoxes in morphology and on the lexicon/syntax boundary' (1988a: 321) with liberal type-shifting and a non-harmonic composition (or, equivalently, division) rule. His morphological examples have been mentioned above (Ch.5.ii). Syntactic examples include verb raising in German and Dutch: the word order and orientation of functors in German raised verb clusters are amenable to conventional, Lambek-valid harmonic composition, but Dutch shows the mirror-image and requires the disharmonic form (note the use of Lambek, result-on-top notation, which makes mixed and backwards rules easier to read than result-first):

5.17 (German) $\underline{\text{zu lesen}}$ versuchen   möchte
                 NP\VP   VP\VP   VP\VP
                 ————————————<C
                     NP\VP
                 ————————————————————<C
                         NP\VP

5.18 (Dutch)   wil   proberen $\underline{\text{te lezen}}$
                 VP/VP   VP/VP   NP\VP
                           ————————————XC
                               NP\VP
                 ————————————————————XC
                       NP\VP

                                              (ibid.: 335)

That disharmonic composition is the appropriate mechanism to use here, rather than some form of wrapping, is shown by the possibility of co-ordinating basic with raised verb clusters, which must therefore have identical categories:

5.19

dat ik een inbreker neerstak   maar daarna liet ontsnappen
that I a burglar knocked-down but then   let escape
'that I knocked down a burglar but let him escape afterwards'

dat hij een meisje zag binnenkomen en meteen   omhelsde
that he a girl   saw enter   and immediately embraced
'that he saw a girl come in and embraced her immediately'

                                              (ibid.: 334)

Developing this further, Moortgat (1988b: 85ff.) shows that proto-typical 'peripheral' extractions can be described using a 'harmonic' raising rule (like Steedman's topicalization) $X \Rightarrow Y/(Y/X)$ – a permutation form of Lambek's direction-preserving rule – and Lambek's normal binary rules. For 'non-peripheral' extractions like *I know what John put on the table*, however, disharmonic composition is needed to link *what* to its 'extraction site' between *put* and *on the table*.

> The composition of the extraction domain ... is clearly not a lex-ical matter, so we cannot adopt the proposal of Steedman [1987] to derive the expression *John put on the table* on the basis of type-restricted LP extensions: ... we want to confine type-restricted LP type transitions to the lexicon.
>
> (ibid.: 113)

His solution makes use of the infixation connectives discussed above (Ch.4.ii), assigning lexically to the extracted wh-word, in this case, the category $S/(S{\uparrow}NP)$, 'a lifted second order type, which requires to its right an incomplete S expression with an NP missing somewhere' (ibid.).

Moortgat himself recognizes, indeed proves, that disharmonic com-position licenses permutation closure, another serious case of over-generation. Various devices have been proposed to constrain these over-powerful rules in (relatively) non-*ad-hoc* ways: Steedman (1990: 219) suggests that a bound be stipulated on the recursive depth of generalized function composition equal to the maximum valency found in the lexicon; Moortgat, as we have seen, is in constant quest for an only just linguistically adequate categorial calculus; and both Dowty and Moortgat follow Partee and Rooth (1983) in permitting raising to apply only when and as far as an analysis strictly demands it.

Others take further this move to avoid excessive power by replacing unary rules rather than constraining them. Chierchia (1988), although looking at binding rather than extraction and clearly influenced by his background in Government–Binding theory, claims that 'The use of wrap operations seems to be a crucial ingredient of ... the categorial theory of grammatical relations' (1988: 127), and compares general-ized wrap to 'Move α'. Pareschi (1988) is explicitly critical of Steedman and Moortgat's attempts to constrain in a principled way an inherently over-powerful calculus. Like Moortgat, he distinguishes peripheral extraction, which he agrees is simple enough, from non-peripheral extraction, which raises the problem of discontinuity:

> a solution like the one proposed in [Steedman 1987] involves permuting the arguments of a given function. Such an operation needs to be rather cumbersomely constrained in an explicit way to cases of extraction, lest it should wildly overgenerate. Another solution, proposed in [Moortgat 1987b] is also cumbersome and counter-intuitive, in that it involves the assignment of multiple types to wh-expressions, one for each site where extraction can take place.
>
> (Pareschi 1988: 272)

This is too high a price to pay for adjacency. Instead, exploiting the expressive power of first-order logic,

> we drop all explicit requirements of adjacency between combinable constituents, and we capture word-order constraints simply by allowing subformulae of complex types to share variables ranging over string positions.
>
> (ibid.: 270)

Constructive eclecticism can be found here too. Dowty (1988: 188–9) thoughtfully suggests that, while raising and composition are appropriate for the description of clause-bounded phenomena like non-constituent co-ordination, unbounded phenomena might be better handled with a GPSG-like feature-passing mechanism: after all, 'a complete categorial theory of grammar for natural languages will undoubtedly require a fairly elaborate theory of syntactic features', rich enough to handle unbounded extraction and thus to retain a less powerful basic calculus. Bouma (1987) also questions the integrated treatment of unbounded dependency and co-ordination, giving English and Dutch data which show its predictions to be incorrect, and introduces to a Categorial Unification Grammar a feature-percolation mechanism and 'gap' feature which is again reminiscent of the GPSG account; Morrill (1988) is another interesting CG/GPSG hybrid covering similar data.

Huck (1988), looking at discontinuous phrasal verbs (*look the number up*), distinguishes four types of 'postponement'. 'Argument-postponements' require only simple function composition; 'functor-postponements' can be handled with type-raising; '$-postponements' correspond to the use of generalized composition; and 'minus-feature postponements' look (again) much like the GPSG slash-feature mechanism. Huck places these in order of formal power but claims that all stop short of full context-sensitivity, that is to say, none will generate $a^n b^n c^n$, a language in which all well-formed expressions consist of equal numbers of a, b and c in any order. Pollard (1988: 394) sees the two basic approaches as parallel, wrap and scramble as syntactic and raising and composition as semantic. His own account of long-distance dependency is another to use the 'slash-category' mechanism of GPSG in preference to raising and composition, but he concludes (ibid.: 409) that 'I think the questions of whether there are clearcut computational, empirical, or aesthetic wins for either account are still open.'

In conclusion it is worth touching on two special cases which, although they have received relatively little attention, stretch the limits of the grammar in interesting ways. The first is the class of constructions involving multiple dependencies known as 'parasitic gaps'. As noted above (Ch.4.iii.c), Steedman (1987: 425–6) observes that in a 'parasitic-gap' construction like *articles which I will file__without reading__*, the phrase *file without reading* displays much of the behaviour of a transitive verb, and suggests that it should have the category VP/NP. This assignment can be derived using the syntagmatic rule of 'functional substitution' proposed by Anna Szabolcsi (1983) (referred to there and in Szabolcsi (1987) as 'connection', perhaps a more perspicuous term):

$$Y/Z \ (X\backslash Y)/Z \to X/Z$$

and thus

5.20   file   without reading
    VP/NP ———————————
               (VP\VP)/NP
    ———————————————S
        VP/NP

As with functional composition, four versions of the rule are formally possible, forward and backward harmonic and disharmonic ('crossing': Steedman 1987:427):

(a) $(X/Y)/Z$ $Y/Z \to X/Z$ (forward)
(b) $(X/Y)\backslash Z$ $Y\backslash Z \to X\backslash Z$ (forward crossing)
(c) $Y\backslash Z$ $(X\backslash Y)\backslash Z \to X\backslash Z$ (backward)
(d) Y/Z $(X\backslash Y)/Z \to X/Z$ (backward crossing)

Of these, English is taken to require the use of the backward crossing rule (d), as in the example above, and of the simple forward rule (a) for multiple dependencies in arguments of a verb, such as *men who*(*m*) *I will persuade every friend of to vote for*, the 'rather border-line' *a man whom I will send a picture of to* and the even worse *a man whom I will show to* (ibid.: 20; see also Steedman 1988: 423–9). This is a significant formal step, taking the grammar beyond 'the family of count-invariant calculi' (Moortgat 1988b: 88) by introducing a con-traction rule (see ibid.: 88–90).

The second special case is a notorious one, that of 'crossing' depen-dencies in Dutch – one of the very few known natural language con-structions provably to require context-sensitive power for its description. Natural languages overwhelmingly adhere to Fodor's (1978) 'Nested Dependency Constraint' – if a sentence includes more than one discontinuous dependency, they will be embedded, not inter-sected (*The tap$_1$ the plumber$_2$ your mother$_3$ recommended$_3$ fitted$_2$ leaks$_1$*). Bach (1977), Fodor (1978) and Ades and Steedman (1982) all comment that this is what one would expect if the processor uses a stack, a last-in first-out strategy for matching the separated related items, as in the computational parsing of context-free formal lan-guages (more on the psychological plausibility of this below, Ch. 6.iii). In Dutch, however, such constructions show intersecting dependencies:

5.21(a)
... omdat   ik$_1$ Cecilia$_2$ de nijlpaarden$_2$ zag$_1$ voeren$_2$
... because I   Cecilia the hippos   saw feed
... 'because I saw Cecilia feed the hippos'

5.21(b)
... omdat   ik$_1$ Cecilia$_2$ Henk$_3$ de nijlpaarden$_3$ zag$_1$ helpen$_2$ voeren$_3$
... because I   Cecilia Henk the hippos   saw help   feed
... 'because I saw Cecilia help Henk feed the hippos'

(Steedman 1985a: 524)

Characteristically, Steedman (1985a) uses generalized composition to derive the verb group as a functor which works backwards by applica-tion through the noun group to produce a finite verb phrase and then an embedded sentence; Moortgat (1988b) builds the verb group by dis-harmonic composition, as shown above (Ch. 5.iii.4.b); and Bach (1984) accounts for the surface order with wrapping rules. Bresnan *et al.*'s (1982) LFG account of the same phenomenon makes an interesting contrast. The reader is referred to the original sources for details, and may pick according to preference: here as for the wider question, the jury is likely to remain out for some time.

5.iii.d Co-ordination

Co-ordinate constructions have proved to be amongst the most resistant of all natural language phenomena to graceful formalization in the dominant tradition of phrase-structure grammars. The observed structures of naturally occurring conjuncts do not, on the whole, correspond well to the hypothetical structures of phrase-structure trees; witness the wide range of 'non-constituent' co-ordinations. What conjuncts do correspond to, not only in English but as a cross-linguistic generalization, is continuous segments of the surface order of grammatical sentences. In other words, co-ordination appears to be not a structural, but a linear phenomenon.

There is a long and distinguished tradition of addressing categorial grammars to co-ordinate constructions: the first full natural language sentence to be given a CG derivation (in Ajdukiewicz 1935) is co-ordinated, and the 'program for syntax' set out in Geach (1972) looks carefully at co-ordination. This is so richly packed and finely judged a summary of central issues and elegant solutions that no abbreviated recapitulation can do it justice. Briefly, however, Geach assigns to subordinating conjunctions the category ::sss (equivalent to $(S|S)|S$), a function from a sentence to a modifier of a sentence; a co-ordinating conjunction is :s(2s) $(S|(S*S))$, a function from two sentences to a sentence. He goes on:

> Grammarians have often taken sentences in which a co-ordinating connective joins expressions other than sentences to be derived from sentences in which the same connective joins sentences. I regard this view as wholly erroneous. Our theory of categories does not restrict the possible arguments of an :s(2s) connective to a pair of sentences; on the contrary, by our recursive rule [of division] we have that a pair of the category :sb $[S|X]$ may also be so connected to form a third:

> Since :s(2s) s s → s, :s(2s) :sb :sb → :sb,
>   whatever category **b** may be.

And so we obtain a correct analysis of a sentence like:

> *All the girls admired, but most boys detested, one of the saxophonists.*

This is not equivalent, as a moment's thought shows, to:

> *All the girls admired one of the saxophonists, but most boys detested one of the saxophonists,*

and cannot sensibly be regarded as a transformation of it. The expressions *all the girls admired* and *most boys detested* are in fact each assignable to the category **:sn** [S|N] ... so the co-ordinating connective *but* can combine them to form a single string of category **:sn**.

(ibid.: 487–8)

There are good recent discussions in (among others) Dowty (1988), Morrill (1988), Wood (1989) and Steedman (1985a, 1990). Non-constituent co-ordination has remained the focus of particular interest – not surprisingly, since here the flexible 'constituency' offered by a generalized CG gives it a distinctive advantage over fixed-constituent-structure grammars. I will try here to summarize the essentials of Steedman (1985a), Dowty (1988) and Wood (1989).

An important influence on all these has been Gazdar's (1980) squib 'A cross-categorial semantics for co-ordination', which for the first time provided an explicit (Montagovian) semantic interpretation for a co-ordination rule schema which used a variable to generalize across categories. The schema formalizes the observation that a string of any syntactic category can be made up of two or more substrings of that same category, appropriately linked by a conjunction, which in English appears in pre-final position:

$$\alpha \rightarrow \alpha_1 \ ... \ \beta\alpha_n$$

where $2 \leqslant n$, $\beta \in \{and, or\}$, and α is any syntactic category.

(1980: 407)

and its semantics says that a co-ordinate structure is to be interpreted as the intersection (for conjunction) or union (for disjunction) of the interpretations of the conjuncts. Something like this schema is the basis for most (although not all) current CG accounts of co-ordination, and its variable-based polymorphism is, as far as I know, now unanimously accepted.

Gazdar's (1981) syntax for co-ordination again offers an instructive contrast to the possibilities in CG. Take the prototypical problem case, 'right node raising' (rnr), where (as in his account of unbounded dependency, to which it is closely related) the slash feature is critical. For a sentence like *Harry caught and Mary killed the rabid dog*, previous phrase-structure accounts, unable to accept the subject—verb substrings as constituents, had to posit deletion from an underlying sentential co-ordination *Harry caught the rabid dog and Mary killed the rabid dog*. The slash feature allows Gazdar to express this as co-ordination simply of the subject—verb conjuncts with traces holding the places of the object:

5.22

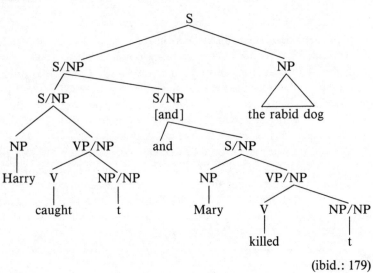

(ibid.: 179)

For elegance and economy this is a vast improvement on previous phrase-structure accounts. But the grammar of Ades and Steedman (1982) already included all that is needed for an entirely direct and simple description of rnr sentences. By raising the subject from **NP** to **S/(S\NP)** and composing it with the transitive verb category **(S\NP)/NP** – as we wish to do anyway, for the sake of incremental interpretation – we can derive for each conjunct the category **S/NP**, and can therefore conjoin them. (The category system of Steedman (1985a) is non-directional, but that does not affect the principle.)

Speaking personally for a moment, it was my first sight of this derivation which won me over conclusively to CG, and I still find it a model of linguistic elegance and a thing of real beauty:

5.23

Harry	cooked	and	Mary	ate	the	beans
S/(S\NP)	(S\NP)/NP	conj	S/(S\NP)	(S\NP)/NP	NP/N	N

$$
\begin{array}{ccccc}
\text{Harry} & \text{cooked} & \text{and} & \text{Mary} & \text{ate} & \text{the} & \text{beans} \\
\text{S/(S\backslash NP)} & \text{(S\backslash NP)/NP} & \text{conj} & \text{S/(S\backslash NP)} & \text{(S\backslash NP)/NP} & \text{NP/N} & \text{N}
\end{array}
$$

———————>C ———————————>C———————>A
   S/NP   S/NP   NP
 <———————— & ——————————>
        S/NP
                                  ———————————————>A
                       S

(after Steedman 1985a: 641)

'Conj' is a shorthand for a Gazdar-like 'phrase-structure rule schema'

$$X^{+} \text{ conj } X \Rightarrow X$$

where 'X stands as usual for any category, whether atomic or a functor. The superscript " + " means "one or more" and "conj" stands for conjunctions like *and*' (ibid.: 540). This essentially very simple rule, together with the raising-and-composition account of unbounded dependency described earlier, is shown to handle cleanly such complex English examples as *To which woman **did Harry offer**, **and will Mary actually give**, an autographed copy of Syntactic Structures?* or *Harry **sold Barry** and **Don gave John** the bicycles that they stole from Mary*, and Dutch examples of at least comparable complexity. The connection between co-ordination and extraction is shown by the parallel between, for example, *beans which **Harry cooked and Mary ate** / **Harry cooked and Mary ate** the beans I bought from Alice*, again with comparable data from Dutch.

Dowty (1988) develops further the use of raising and function composition for the CG description of non-constituent co-ordination. A 'basic' grammar including only function application would generate all and only 'normal' constituent structures, when those were needed; an 'extended' grammar, adding composition, raising, extraction-licensing categories and so on would provide the non-standard structures found in unbounded dependency and non-constituent co-ordination. These structures, such as the subject–verb conjuncts found in right node raising, he calls 'phantom constituents'. Type-raising (discussed at length) and harmonic composition are shown not to extend the weak, but only the strong generative power of the basic grammar; but this is not true of the extended grammar, where a wide range of strange co-ordinate constructions become tractable.

Adopting Steedman's co-ordination schema [X⁺ Conj X] = X 'for simplicity', Dowty (1988: 170) shows that the combination of object-raising and backward harmonic composition offers a natural account of non-constituent co-ordination (a term which he restricts to con-structions 'with incomplete conjuncts on the right and "shared" material on the left') — for example (ibid.):

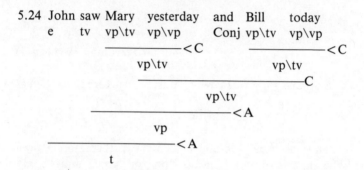

Notice that the objects must be raised (as explained above, Ch. 3.iv) for composition to build the object-plus-postmodifier 'phantom con-stituent' conjuncts; that is, raising is needed for syntactic, but not semantic, reasons.

The case of a ditransitive construction with conjoined paired objects has a controversial history, Gazdar (1981) having treated it as an instance of verb gapping, while Hudson (1982) takes the conjuncts to be 'complete'. Here (Dowty 1988: 171–2) and in Steedman (1990: 228) the paired objects are raised and then combined by back-ward composition, their resulting category being that of a functor looking backwards for a ditransitive verb to return a verb phrase; this also ensures the correct semantic interpretation:

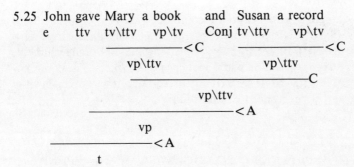

5.25

More complex examples, where one element of each conjunct is, as Dowty terms it, a 'partial sub-constituent' – *John went to Chicago on Monday and Detroit on Tuesday* – are also naturally covered by object and verb raising and backward composition (ibid.: 176–9). Apart from the move to a directional category system, Dowty's proposals were complementary to Steedman's, and indeed were largely taken up in Steedman (1990), which I will look at in the discussion of gapping in the next section.

A somewhat different approach to the same data is taken in Wood (1989). The grammar here includes simple forward composition but not the generalized or backward forms, and raising only for subjects; conjunction is handled by a polymorphic functor category, rather than by a phrase-structure-like schema. Wood aims to show that by using the product connective (see Ch.4.ii above), and allowing functor categories to take products as their arguments, this less powerful calculus is adequate for most types of non-constituent co-ordination.

The 'schema' for conjunction adopted by Steedman and Dowty sits uneasily in a CG, as they both admit. The obvious alternative is a polymorphic functor $(X\backslash X)/X$, which would apply first to something on its right, then on its left to give a result of the same category. Wood argues that this nested pattern is indeed appropriate to subordinating conjunction, but that co-ordinating conjunction should apply flatly, to both conjuncts at once. This can be done with an 'un-curried' or 'flattened' functor which applies by infixation to a product argument: thus $XI(X^+*X)$, where the Kleene plus has the same effect as in the Gazdar *et al.* schema.

Steedman's derivation for right node raising is the starting point for the description of non-constituent co-ordination, but to extend it to the analogous ditransitive construction is problematic. The raised subject category **S/(S\NP)** can combine with the transitive verb category **(S\NP)/NP** by simple composition. The ditransitive verb category **((S\NP)/PP)/NP**, however, having an additional argument, must have a corresponding additional layer of brackets. The combination **S/(S\NP) ((S\NP)/PP)/NP** then requires, not simple, but the more powerful generalized composition:

5.26

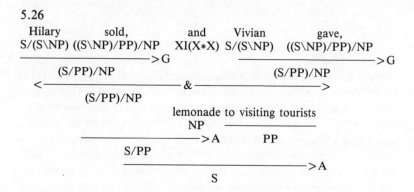

If the verb is assigned its flattened category, as explained above, looking for a product of two arguments (its two objects) as its one following argument, simple composition is enough to combine it with its subject:

5.27

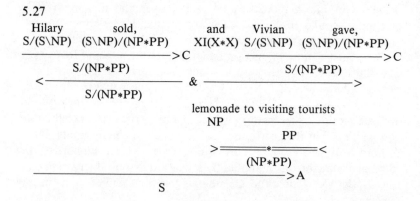

As a further consequence, co-ordination of paired ditransitive objects is straightforward. Rather than requiring object-raising and backwards composition as in Dowty's and Steedman's accounts, the objects are combined by product formation, co-ordinated, and then combined by application with the subject-plus-flattened-verb category:

5.28

Chris	gave	a dog	a bone	and	a policeman	a flower
S/(S\NP)	(S\NP)/(NP*NP)	——	——	XI(X*X)	——	——

$$
\begin{array}{c}
\underline{\hspace{4cm}} >C \quad NP \quad NP \qquad\qquad NP \quad NP \\
S/(NP*NP) \qquad >\!\!==\!\!*\!\!==\!\!< \qquad >\!\!==\!\!*\!\!==\!\!< \\
(NP*NP) \qquad\qquad (NP*NP) \\
<\!\!\underline{\hspace{3cm}} \; \& \; \underline{\hspace{3cm}}\!\!> \\
(NP*NP) \\
\underline{\hspace{7cm}} >A \\
S
\end{array}
$$

This is, of course, only a quick sketch − all these proposals, and others which I have not considered here, are more complex and detailed than this suggests. There are plenty of problems still to be solved, even allowing the degree of broad consensus among these three accounts: Barry and Pickering (1990), for example, is an illuminating discussion of the internal structure(s) and dependency relations of English conjuncts. There are distinctive insights to be gained from work on GPSG hybrids (e.g. Morrill 1988), and from the rich Dutch tradition of semantically and algebraically based research (e.g. Hendriks 1987). Cross-typological work is needed, too. But the work that has been done looks intelligent, and the prospects for its further development look good.

5.iii.e Gapping

The problems of co-ordination and of discontinuity are both shown by sentence co-ordinations where the verb in the second sentence is missing: *Michael keeps a pet rat, and Chris goldfish.* Phrase-structure accounts generally derive these 'gapped' constructions by deletion from an underlying form with two verbs, and/or posit some sort of phonologically unrealized anaphor in place of the 'missing' verb. Thus Ross (1970: 250) speaks of

> the English rule of GAPPING, which converts structures under-
> lying such sentences as those in (1) into those underlying the
> corresponding sentences in (2).

> (1) (a) I ate fish, Bill ate rice, and Harry ate roast beef.
> ...
> (2) (a) I ate fish, Bill rice, and Harry roast beef.

Clearly, this approach is not compatible with the principles of CG. I will look here at three rather different CG proposals which have been put forward: Wood (1989) reconstructs from the subject and object 'remnants' the category of the gap and matches it to that of its antecedent; Steedman (1990) further extends raising and composition to treat the remnants together as a constituent; and Oehrle (1987) shows that, at least in some cases, scope relations show that the second conjunct cannot be genuinely 'gapped'.

The grammar of Wood (1989) stipulates that backward combination rules can only operate with endocentric functor categories (in which the result is of the same category as the argument, for example adjectives (**N/N**), adverbs (**VP\VP**) and prepositional phrases (**N\N**): *the fat cat*, *run quickly*, *the cat on the mat*. In exocentric categories, the argument and result differ – **S\NP**, **(S\NP)/NP**, **NP/N**, etc.). In a sequence of category specifications which offer a complete and well-formed left-to-right derivation, the principal slash operator in each exocentric category (and, in practice, many of the endocentric categories also) will look to the right for its argument. Further, the right-hand, argument element of each complex category must match the left-hand, result element of the category following.

There is thus a chaining relation throughout any grammatical string. This can be illustrated by a simple example:

5.29 Michael   keeps   a   pet   rat
   S / (S\NP)   (S\NP) / NP   NP / N   N / N   N

For a sentence involving verb gapping, this chaining relation breaks down at the gap:

5.30

Michael	keeps	a	pet	rat	and	Chris __ goldfish
S/(S\NP)	(S\NP)/NP	NP/N	N/N	N	XI(X^{+}*X)	S/(S\NP) NP

The missing item in such a string can be automatically determined by completing the chain, reconstituting the category necessary to link the items on either side. This category must have as its left-hand, result element the right-hand, argument element of the category on its left; and, as its right-hand, argument element the result of the category on its right. In this example, the reconstituted category will be (S\NP)/NP. Wood (1989: 228–59) shows that a range of less straightforward cases can also be handled this way.

This makes the syntactic pattern coherent, but not, in itself, the semantic interpretation. There must also be some item or substring earlier in the sentence which is of this category, which will be interpreted as the intended or understood 'filler' for the gap (in this instance, *keeps*). Categorial identity appears to be a necessary but not a sufficient condition on the antecedent of a reconstituted category: Kuno (1976) gives a number of examples with more than one syntactically plausible interpretation of which only one is in fact possible, due to various extrasyntactic factors. While these can reasonably be left beyond the scope of a bare syntactic analysis, a more serious problem with this proposal is that its suggestion of a 'real' gap, filled in semantic interpretation by anaphora, is not really in keeping with CG's commitment to observed surface structures.

Steedman (1990), on the other hand, is able to treat gapping as 'constituent co-ordination', but at the cost of using a relatively elaborate grammar. To capture gapped constructions in the same co-ordination rule as any other conjoined construction, they must be analysed as having two (or more) 'constituents' − that is, two continuous surface substrings with the same (lexical or derived) category specification − with a co-ordinating conjunction (*and*, *or*) between them. This analysis is reached in two steps: firstly, determining what category the second, 'gapped' conjunct can have as a 'constituent'; and secondly finding a constituent of that category in the first, 'complete' conjunct. In the example above, the right conjunct *Chris goldfish* must first be given a single category, and then a substring of that same category must be found in the left conjunct *Michael keeps a pet rat* to match it, so that the co-ordination rule can apply in the usual way.

The first of these steps requires forward disharmonic composition, constrained to apply only to a function into VP, that is, a type-raised object category or a VP modifier, in a right conjunct (conjuncts are marked by the subscript '&'; B denotes the combinator for composition; see Ch.4.iv above):

$$[X/Y]_\& \ Y\backslash Z \Rightarrow_B [X\backslash Z]_\&$$
$$\text{where } Y = S\backslash NP$$

(Steedman 1990: 235)

allowing derivations like (T indicates type-raising):

5.31

Harry eats beans, and	Barry	potatoes

conj ————> T   —————————————— < T

S/(S\NP)   (S\NP)\((S\NP)/NP)

————————> &

[S/(S\NP)] &

————————————————————————— > Bx

[S\((S\NP)/NP)] &

(ibid.)

The second step, finding such a constituent in the first conjunct, uses a rule of 'decomposition' – in effect, a division rule, based on the reversibility, or 'parametric neutrality', of categorial composition first explored by Pareschi (1986) and Pareschi and Steedman (1987). 'Specifying any two categories that are related by a given binary combinatory rule determines the third' (Steedman 1990: 238). While combinatory rules are normally thought of as having the two constituent elements as input and returning their composed category as output, knowing the category of a complete string and of one of its components equally gives the category of the remainder, or complement:

$$a \mid b \; b \rightarrow X \; \Rightarrow X = a$$
$$a \mid b \; X \rightarrow a \; \Rightarrow X = b$$
$$X \; b \rightarrow a \; \Rightarrow X = a \mid b$$

(The second case could also return $a \mid (a \mid b)$, but this is simply **b** raised over **a**, and so not a damaging counter-example.) The third case is the one of particular interest. Given a string of category **a** within which there is a substring of category **b**, the remainder must be of category $a \mid b$. In other words, the category of the larger item is divided by the category of its subset to derive the category of the complement.

Decomposition abstracts away from the original word order within the decomposed category. Crucially, however, although its word order is not respected, its semantic interpretation is, blocking the generation of indefinite numbers of spurious decompositions. If **A** could, given its semantic interpretation and context, have been derived from either **A** | **X**, **X** or **A** | **Y**, **Y** – if both **X** and **Y**, but not **Z**, are available at some level of interpretation – then, regardless of how it actually was derived, decomposition will be able to return either of those sequences, but not **A|Z,Z**. This is expressed in the constraints on Steedman's 'Left Conjunct Revealing Rule':

$$X \Rightarrow Y \; X\backslash Y$$
$$\text{where } X = S$$
$$\text{and } Y = \text{given}(X)$$

(1990: 250)

We can now complete the partial derivation above:

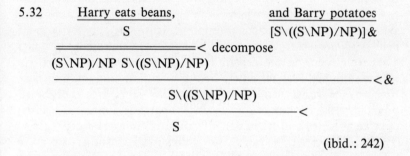

5.32

ibid.: 242)

Abstracting away from word order − finessing adjacency − makes the problem of discontinuous gaps unproblematic: *Harry wants Ipswich to win, and Barry, Watford* has a derivation effectively identical to the one above. Cases to which the grammar might otherwise over-generate, such as **Harry ran, and Mary, quickly* (on the intended reading) are blocked by the need for contextual support.

Notice that Pareschi and Steedman's decomposition is very similar, formally, to Wood's reconstitution. The principal difference between them is that decomposition determines the category of an existing surface string between two given points, while reconstitution determines that of a gap between two points. The principle is essentially the same. The analyses of gapping based on them are, however, very different, and the choice between them may well be a choice of the lesser evil: real gaps in a restricted calculus, or real constituents in a complex and extrinsically constrained one?

Oehrle's (1987) work weighs in against gaps, although not necessarily in favour of complex composition rules. He notes that some 'gapped' sentences have an element with wide scope properly contained within the first conjunct. Compare the interpretations of:

5.33 (a) Mrs J can't live in Boston and Mr J in LA.
     (b) Mrs J can't live in Boston and Mr J can't live in LA.
     (c) Mrs J can't live in Boston or Mr J in LA.
     (d) Mrs J can't live in Boston or Mr J can't live in LA.

(1987: 205)

If the negation here has narrow scope relative to the connectives – that is, holds within each separate conjunct, so that the connective joins two independently negated items – a GPSG or similar account of both syntax and semantics can cope with these. However, only with a great deal of *ad hoc* feature passing could it handle the interpretation which gives wide scope to the negation. On these readings, (a) is closely related (although not absolutely equivalent) to (d), and (c) equivalent to (b), by the De Morgan Laws. An account of gapped sentences based on ungapped analogues would predict, conversely, that (a) should be equivalent to (b) and (c) to (d). Clearly, something else is needed.

Oehrle points out the flexibility of derivational constituent structure offered by a generalized categorial grammar, and the close relation of this flexibility to a general theory of co-ordination. Specifically, his analysis of gapping makes crucial use of structures produced by 'allow[ing] functions to act on pairs, triples, and, in general, *n*-tuples of arguments, rather than simply on a single argument' (ibid.: 209), and on the ability of the Boolean connectives *and* and *or* to conjoin these *n*-tuples. In practice, he does not use the full generality of this initial formulation, but only 'the Cartesian product NP × NP', ordered pairs of NPs – these are effectively Lambek's products (see Ch. 4.ii above), restricted to NPs. The closure of the set of these products under the binary operations 'meet' and 'join' (in other words, all possible pairs of NPs in a given language conjoined by *and* ('meet') or *or* ('join')), referred to as $L[NP \times NP]$, has the structure of a distributive lattice or a Boolean algebra (although not the syntactic properties of idempotence and commutativity – *beans and rice* is not the same NP as *rice and beans*).

> Thus, if *Kim, the beans, Sandy,* and *the rice* belong to category NP, then ⟨*Kim, the beans*⟩ and ⟨*Sandy, the rice*⟩ are members of the Cartesian product NP × NP, and the meet ⟨*Kim, the rice*⟩ *and* ⟨*Sandy, the beans*⟩ belongs to $L[NP \times NP]$.
>
> (ibid.: 210)

A verb like *eat* can take this conjunction of products as its argument, with a phonological action under which it is realized only in the first conjunct and a semantic action under which it applies to both, leading to a simple gapped sentence like *Kim ate the beans and Sandy the rice*. Formally, the phonological action f^* works on lattice structures thus:

> If $x \in L[NP \times NP]$ and there are z and w in $L[NP \times NP]$ such that $x = (zw)$, then $f^*(x) = f^*(z)$ *and* w.

(ibid.: 222)

In other words, if x is a pair of NPs made up of the conjunction of z and w, themselves each a pair of NPs, then the action of f^* on x is the same as the action of f^* on its first pair, followed by the second.

we can represent the analysis of *Kim ate the beans* in the following way:

$$ate\langle \textbf{Kim, the beans}\rangle$$

...When x is a single pair of NPs, such as $\langle\textbf{Kim, the beans}\rangle$, $ate^*(x) = ate\langle (Kim,\ the\ beans)\rangle = Kim\ ate\ the\ beans$. When x is the meet of two simple pairs, such as $\langle\textbf{Kim, the beans}\rangle$ $\langle\textbf{Sandy, the rice}\rangle$, then $ate^*(x) = ate\langle (Kim,\ the\ beans)\rangle$ *and* *Sandy the rice* = *Kim ate the beans and Sandy the rice*.

(ibid.)

Oehrle's concluding discussion suggests that other forms of non-constituent co-ordination can be handled this way, giving as an example the ditransitive construction *Kim gave the tacos to Sandy and the chimichangas to Les*, where *give* is taken as a function R-gave: $NP \times to\text{-}P\ -\text{>}decS/NP$, that is, from the product of NP and *to*-PP to a predicate or VP. The corresponding lattice function $R\text{-}gave^*:L[NP \times to\text{-}P] \rightarrow decS/NP$ operates similarly on a pair of such products. This is effectively identical to Wood's product-based analysis of the same construction (Ch.5.iii.d above).

The use of products to describe the ⟨subject, object⟩ string in a gapped sentence, allowing an effectively 'non-gapped' analysis, explicitly semantically motivated, may well offer the best of both other possibilities, the relative simplicity of Wood's calculus and the direct surface description of Steedman's account. It is not by coincidence that both these accounts generalize naturally to 'discontinuous gaps', as in *Kim put a gun on the table and Sandy a knife*: this follows from the abstraction away from word order which is needed to derive an appropriate first conjunct in the simple transitive case. By that same token, however, it is essential that word order and the status of the Adjacency Principle should be fully considered at some point.

6 Current issues

If work in CGs has been patchy in its linguistic coverage, it has been exemplary in its attention to its formal foundations and underlying principles. As the previous chapter has shown, a good deal of categorial linguistic description has been motivated by concerns at this level, and all of it has been respectfully aware of them. In this chapter I will survey quickly the most important of these issues.

Most important − if one had to choose − is the categorial commitment to the centrality of the tight relation between syntax and semantics. If 'Montague Grammar' as such is no longer pursued, many CGs still adopt a Montague semantics. Other semantic systems have also been proposed, notably the combinators of Combinatory Categorial Grammar − the categorial purists respecting the rule-to-rule hypothesis, closely related work adopting a less rigid position − and will be touched on here.

How to specify word order in a CG has been more debated: whether a calculus should be directional at all, and whether directionality should be a property of combination rules, of functors or even of arguments. There are debates, too, as we have seen, about directional constraints on the form of combination rules, and about whether to maintain an adjacency principle or to use wrapping rules in describing discontinuities. Universals, both of underlying structure and of word order, are another concern, related often to issues of psychological plausibility − simple, fundamental constraints on the rule system are argued to predict observed universals and/or to be appropriate to plausible processing mechanisms.

At the formal end of the spectrum of concern, there is a flourishing school of logical and algebraic work, particularly well represented in Buszkowski *et al.* (1988). Related to this is the investigation of the formal complexity of various calculi. Finally, research into computational parsing with CGs has given an important stimulus to the categorial enterprise. All these will be glanced at, rather than looked at closely; in all cases the interested reader is referred to the original sources for further details.

6.i SEMANTICS

The original strict tie of syntax to semantics – the 'rule-to-rule hypothesis' – has remained a distinctive central principle of CGs. Steedman (1988: 417) opens with the statement that 'The attraction of CG as a notation for natural language grammar has always been the direct relation that it embodies between the syntax of a language and an applicative semantics', and similar comments are prominent in virtually every discussion of CGs. This is, of course, in complete contrast to the principle of Autonomy of Syntax still upheld by GB, rather closer to the GPSG and HPSG view of things which does map semantic interpretation to the rules of phrase structure, but taking that view to its natural extreme.

Of course, insisting on a strict homomorphism between syntax and semantics – a direct mapping between (syntactic) categories and (semantic) types – does not mean ignoring the difference in nature and purpose between the two. Nor does the category/type mapping have to be one to one, as witness the validity of unary type-shifting rules. Moortgat (1988b: 221ff.) argues appealingly for a flexible mapping between categories and types, citing quantifier scope as 'a prime example of a phenomenon that has to be dealt with in the *semantic* algebra, without complicating the syntactic derivation' (ibid.; emphasis in the original).

Richard Montague's attempt 'to apply the techniques developed within mathematical logic to the semantics of natural languages' (Dowty *et al.* 1981: ix) was the first to 'offer the hope that [natural language] semantics can be characterized with the same formal rigour and explicitness that transformational approaches have brought to syntax' (ibid.); and thus, as we have seen (Ch.2.iii.c), inspired and informed the wave of categorial research which was known as 'Montague Grammar'. It is well beyond my present remit to introduce truth-conditional model-theoretic possible-world semantics in general, or Montague's proposals in particular – the interested reader is recommended to Dowty *et al.* (1981), deservedly the standard introduction.

Montague semantics, or recognizable evolutions from it, have been adopted by a number of linguistic theories, including LFG and GPSG. CGs, meanwhile, although still strongly associated with Montague semantics, are no longer strictly tied to it. There is a wide space of debate as to the exact semantics to be used (partially surveyed in van Benthem 1987b). The rule-to-rule hypothesis remains fundamental, and ensures that any syntactic system projects a space of possible semantic systems, and that any particular syntactic analysis similarly defines a semantic analysis within any one of those semantic systems. As van Benthem (1987b: 18) comments,

> As is usual in semantics, having one formal framework at once stimulates phantasy in setting up new ones. Although our type-theoretical semantics was couched in terms of standard function hierarchies on base domains, this is by no means the only possible interpretation for Categorial Grammar.

The most serious alternative to the traditional use of a lambda-calculus is the combinatory logic proposed by Steedman (1988) and Szabolcsi (1987). Combinators, as we have seen (Ch.4.iv), are fundamental terms in which the lambda-calculus and indeed all applicative systems can be defined, and also are argued to offer in a principled way exactly the set of operations needed for linguistic description. Combinatory systems have since been adopted by a number of others, notably Kent Wittenburg (e.g. Wittenburg 1987).

Compositional semantics is thus better developed in CG than in most other linguistic theories. However there has been no serious attempt yet to integrate anything beyond a formal compositional semantics into a CG. Even lexical semantics has been largely ignored, with the honourable exception of Dowty (1979a). Certainly, there are no obvious hooks for pragmatics, discourse structure, text grammar, and so on in a categorial system (except in so far as a CUG is free to incorporate features for anything it might wish: UCG does use a derivative of Kamp's Discourse Representation Theory, but apparently for its treatment of quantification and pronoun resolution rather than for anything to do with 'discourse' (Zeevat *et al.* 1987: 202–5; Zeevat 1988: 211–14)). One can easily imagine approximately how to encode a speech act as a function which takes one situation as an argument and produces another as its result: indeed, Gazdar's (1979) *Pragmatics* is a move in that direction, but one which he promptly abandoned, and which no-one else (as far as I know) has taken up since.

This is probably the last major area left completely untouched by categorial investigation, and clearly will have to be addressed sooner or later. Perhaps a formalization of discourse 'function' along the lines developed by Systemic-Functional Grammar (Halliday 1985) can be indexed to the category variants which license interrogatives, imperatives and so on. Variables to express aspects of 'situation' – place, time, speaker, etc. – could be added to the interpretation, as in Situation theory (Barwise and Perry 1983), followed by HPSG. The range of possibilities is, if anything, even wider here than for semantics: it is devoutly to be hoped that when work is done on categorial pragmatics it is done with enough agreement to be genuinely constructive.

6.ii WORD ORDER

Where to fit the specification of word order, and constraints on word order, in the design of a categorial calculus has always been a much more open question. (The further issue of capturing word-order universals in a principled way is discussed in the next section.) The early systems, following Ajdukiewicz, were concerned entirely with semantics, and so were happy with non-directional calculi which simply ignored word order. Šaumjan's applicative grammar (for which Šaumjan 1973 and Soboleva 1973 are probably the most accessible sources) distinguishes the 'genotype' language, an abstract, possibly universal model of natural languages and so order-free, from 'phenotype' languages – actual existing natural languages – for which word order must, of course, be specified. Complementation is specified by sets, rather than (ordered) strings, in a way strongly reminiscent of current practice in GPSG and HPSG (see below). It is this proposal which Chomsky (1965: 124–5) cursorily dismisses in favour of 'concatenation' rules.

Lambek was the first in the western tradition to attempt syntactic description in a CG, and therefore to introduce directionality, using the directional slash connectives in functor categories which have remained the most common format ever since. Bar-Hillel first experimented with a somewhat different notation: recall the derivation (quoted in Ch.2.iii.b above)

2.1 John   knew   that   Paul   was   a   poor man
    n   s/(n)[n] n/[s]   n   s/(n)[n] n/[n] n/[n]   n

in which the slash is non-directional, and the arguments carry positional markings, square brackets if the argument is to follow the functor, round brackets if it must come before it. He soon gave this up in favour of Lambek's notation, but the difference is more than 'merely' notational – there is a real question as to whether directionality should be seen as a property of the functor or of the arguments.

The former is generally assumed, but Steedman now (1990: fn. 3) argues for the latter, and we have seen it used in Unification Categorial Grammar (Ch. 4.v).

The third possibility is that directionality should not be a property of categories at all, but rather of the combination rules. This is the position taken in Ades and Steedman (1982) and Steedman (1985a), where functions are order-neutral 'as befits their basically semantic nature' (Ades and Steedman 1982: 523). A further advantage of such a system, not explicitly mentioned in the text although it was noticed at the time (Steedman, p.c.), is that it offers a clear separation of valency, given by the category system, and word order, given by the combination rules, comparable to the ID/LP format of GPSG and (later) HPSG. This has been abandoned in Steedman's later work, but it remains appealing in principle, and is probably necessary for the description of free-word-order languages.

It is thus not surprising to find a number of CG/GPSG hybrids looking explicitly to integrate an ID/LP distinction with a categorial base. Foster (1990) is a good example, motivated by the demands of describing semi-free word order in Spanish. Hepple's (1990) proposal to separate the specification of the order of arguments from the position of their head among them is also somewhat similar; he suggests that it may be particularly useful for the description of the Germanic 'verb-second' constraint. Steele's (1988) account of argument structure as a grammatical unit also comes to mind. In Flynn (1983), 'Categorial assignment determines hierarchical organization of phrases universally, and specification of precedence relations (for languages which have restrictions) is provided by a single, simple principle, called the word order convention' (ibid.: 141), and Hoeksema's (1985) morphology takes a similar position.

These remain in the minority, however, and most recent CG work uses directional functor categories. These raise problems of their own, as we have seen, regarding the degrees of freedom available to directionality. Steedman (1990: 225) states three principles which are claimed to be universal constraints on combinatory rules:

The Principle of Adjacency: Combinatory rules may only apply to entities which are linguistically realized and adjacent.

The Principle of Directional Consistency: All syntactic combinatory rules must be consistent with the directionality of the principal function.

The Principle of Directional Inheritance: If the category that results from the application of a combinatory rule is a function category, then the slash defining directionality for a given argument in that category will be the same as the one defining directionality for the corresponding argument(s) in the input function(s).

We will return to adjacency shortly. Consistency and inheritance are not questioned, but even they allow the disharmonic or 'crossing' composition and raising rules which license permutation closure: more parsimonious grammars (e.g. Dowty 1988; Wood 1989) include only harmonic rules, but do not necessarily cover as wide a range of data. Bouma's (1986a, 1986b) analysis of Warlpiri uses harmonic combination rules, but with directionally neutral category variants and a unary rule of transitivity to allow the description of free word order.

Adjacency, as we have seen, is one of the major contested points within CG. The principle that 'combinatory rules may only apply to entities which are linguistically realized and adjacent' seems intuitively natural and appealing, but faced with discontinuities in real language, it forces the use of a calculus of excessive intrinsic power, which must then be kept in check by extrinsic constraints and filters. The use of wrapping rules, giving up adjacency, has seemed preferable to a number of categorial grammarians, whether based on the model of transformational movement rules (Bach), on the order-free nature of the underlying logic (thus Pareschi 1988 uses integer indices on strings to specify the elements of discontinuous constituents), or simply concluding that the adjacency principle was not worth its cost in constraints ('No theory is fully satisfactory if it requires ad hoc constraints' – Steedman 1985b: 360). The debate shows no sign of an immediate resolution, and is likely to remain – if one is honest – a matter for subjective preference for some time to come.

6.iii LANGUAGE UNIVERSALS AND PSYCHOLOGICAL PLAUSIBILITY

Any consideration of word order in a grammar leads naturally to the question of language universals. CGs have been argued elegantly to capture, indeed predict, universals of underlying structure and of surface word order, and particular aspects of language variation. For example, Flynn (1983), as we have seen, uses non-directional categories to give a universal statement of the 'hierarchical organization of phrases', with language-specific word-order conventions. This is similar to Dowty's attractive and influential (1982) suggestion that grammatical relations should be universally defined and determined by the order in which arguments combine with their functors. Quoting Montague's syntactic rules

S1: $\langle F_1, \langle IV,T \rangle, t \rangle$ (Subject–Predicate Rule)
S2: $\langle F_2, \langle TV,T \rangle, IV \rangle$ (Verb–Direct-Object Rule)

(where the first member of each triple names a syntactic operation, the second the input string of categories, and the third the output category), he proposes that it is these which

> give us the universal definitions of relations like *Subject-of* and *Object-of*. That is, we will define any term phrase in any language that is combined with an **IV** via S1 as a subject term, and any term phrase that is combined with a **TV** via S2 as a direct object; moreover, these are language independent semantic definitions as well, since the semantic rules corresponding to S1 and S2 will be the same in each language. The manifestation of these relationships in the morphology and word order of a language is what differs from language to language.
>
> (Dowty 1982: 87)

This can form the basis for universal definitions of relations like active/passive, where the passive form is the active stripped of its outermost argument, as in Keenan and Timberlake (1988: see Ch.5.iii.a above).

It has also been claimed that universals of surface order are predicted by certain categorial systems. The earliest such claim that I know of is that of Vennemann and Harlow (1977), who show – in a highly formal, but linguistically sensitive, way – that a language with 'consistent basic *VX* serialization', that is, one which is typologically pure along the lines of Greenberg (1963), strictly head-initial or head-final, can effectively be described with a single categorial rule. They illustrate this with a basic grammar for the VSO (Verb–Subject–Object) language Maori.

More recent, better known and more complex – naturally enough, as the data are more complex too – are the observations of Dowty (1988) developed by Steedman (1990) on the patterns of 'gapping' found in different language types. Dowty, noting that gapping in English remained an outstanding problem for his account of non-constituent co-ordination, observed that

> Gapping *could* be analyzed as a species of non-constituent [co-ordination] in VSO and SOV languages in the present approach,

as long as the order of gapped and whole clauses is (72) in the first case and (73) in the second:

(72) V S O (Conj) S O
(73) S O (Conj) S O V

But of course, it was pointed out in Ross (1970) that exactly these orders of gapped and whole clauses appear to be universal properties of VSO and SOV languages!

(1988: 191–2)

Steedman took up the challenge, producing the analysis of 'gapping as constituent coordination' outlined above (Ch.5.iii.e). Central to that analysis is the argument that the three simple, fundamental constraints on the rule system cited above – the principles of adjacency, directional consistency and directional inheritance – allow all and only the forms of composition and raising which predict the observed universals of gapping. For the details of why this should be so, the reader is referred to the original; it is an impressive enterprise.

Appeals to language-universality often, naturally, run in harness with appeals to psychological plausibility, and it is no different in CG. Claims that particular categorial grammars are appropriate to particular plausible processing mechanisms have been advanced again primarily by Mark Steedman, even as early as Ades and Steedman (1982), where it is already pointed out (as we have seen) that a CG with type-raising and composition allows even unbounded dependencies to be processed incrementally, left to right, in the way that we know is characteristic of the human language processor. The Nested Dependency Constraint (see Ch.5.iii.c above) 'would be predicted by a left-to-right processor that placed preposed constituents into a Push Down Store or stack, and restored them later to their underlying positions' (Ades and Steedman 1982: 521). CG is distinctively suited to such a processor, which can 'build semantic interpretations immediately ... [and] evaluate subexpressions while the analysis is still in progress' (ibid.: 522), again as the human processor does.

The clearest statement of the psycholinguistic issues can be found in Steedman's (1985b) review of the principal LFG source, *The Mental Representation of Grammatical Relations* (Bresnan 1982). LFG remains one of the linguistic theories to take most seriously psychological questions like processing and learnability, developing the Base Generation Hypothesis into a lexically driven model with attractive implications for a model of competence. Bresnan and Kaplan (1982) put forward the 'Strong Competence Hypothesis', which 'demands a theory in which there is a rule-to-rule mapping between syntactic rules, rules of semantic interpretation, and operations of the processor. Such a theory must be base generative in a very strong sense indeed' (Steedman 1985b: 376). Steedman stresses that so little is known about human language processing that it is impossible as yet for such criteria to weigh definitively in favour of any one linguistic theory against all others:

> The strong competence hypothesis is attractive because it implies fewest additional assumptions. However, it is important to remember that it is only a working hypothesis. There is probably no conceivable data that could be used to test it. It can therefore never do more for us than any other instance of Occam's razor – that is, than allow us to choose between theories that are otherwise linguistically adequate.
>
> (ibid.: 361)

In so far as we do judge by its terms, however, it will be clear that CG meets the specification at least as fully as any other current linguistic theory.

On one final point, however, the current state of CG leaves rather more to be desired. 'A grammar that is adequate under the Competence Hypothesis requires nothing more to make a processor than the addition of a mechanism to resolve local ambiguities and decide *which* rules to apply and when' (ibid.: 377). As far as I know, CG nowhere addresses this question from a psychological perspective. There is a good deal of work on computational processing ambiguities (see Ch.6.vi below), but nothing on the mechanisms used by the human language processor to deal with either local or global ambiguities. Crain and Steedman (1985) demonstrate the importance of discourse context in resolving garden-path sentences, remaining theory-neutral, and CGs can certainly go some way by adopting compatible work from a more general framework. But proposals comparable in detail and specificity to Ford *et al.*'s (1982) for LFG would be a valuable contribution to the field.

6.iv LOGIC

If the names of Ajdukiewicz and Montague appear among the references in virtually every CG publication, it is not (just) because workers in CG take a lively pride in their intellectual ancestry, but because the philosophical issues which they address remain live issues, and the logical tradition still flourishes. Formal philosophy of language underpins the concepts of function and argument and the compositional semantics which is so central to CG, and work on logic in various forms continues to feed the categorial mainstream. Buszkowski *et al.* (1988) bear particularly clear witness to the richness of this vein, and a number of papers in Oehrle *et al.* (1988) – notably those by van Benthem, Casadio and Moortgat – are at home here too.

The 'Chronicle of categorial grammar' with which Marciszewski introduces Buszkowski *et al.* (1988: 7–21) is particularly interesting in giving a logician's view of the development and significant distinctive features of CG:

> This fertility in generating ever new functor categories, according to a well-defined mechanism, is similar to the power of the theory of types to embrace the infinity of logical types. This resemblance is by no means accidental; it was intended by S. Leśniewski as the founder of the theory of semantic categories. ... In another respect, the history goes back to Frege's idea of predicate logic as semantically based on the distinction of object and function.
>
> (ibid.: 7)

The importance of Frege's work to the development of logic was noted above (Ch.2.iii.a); Casadio (1988: 109–12) stresses the linguistic relevance of both points, especially as developed by Geach.

The importance of type theory is by no means limited to CG: Klein and Sag's (1985) paper on 'type-driven translation' has been influential throughout the linguistic community. The closeness of the tie between (semantic) types and (syntactic) categories is, however, closer in CG than in other theories, and type theory is correspondingly more important a contributor. Similarly, the fundamental commitment to an integral compositional semantics in CG gives logical approaches to compositional semantics a particular significance (see Buszkowski 1988b, especially Part 4, for a good formally oriented discussion). It is characteristic of CG that the distinctive logic of combinators (Curry and Feys 1958) should have inspired and informed a distinctive school of natural language description (see Ch.4.iv above).

Current research in this area is especially strong in eastern Europe – continuing the strong tradition of Polish logic – and in the Netherlands, led by van Benthem and his colleagues in Amsterdam. Buszkowski *et al.* (1988) is an important collection of new as well as classic work, on the semantics of type-change in a lambda-calculus (van Benthem), the application of higher-order logic and typed lambda-calculus to natural language analysis (Cresswell), the philosophical foundations of (extended) CG (Levin), criteria for the selection of admissible functor–argument structures (Marciszewski), variable-free second-order logic (Došen), 'transparent' higher-order intensional logic with applications to natural language semantics (Materna, Sgall and Hajičová), modifications of Montague's intensional logic and their role in natural language semantics and computational linguistics and a range of similar topics.

The Amsterdam school, led by Johan van Benthem, maintains an impressive output of logically and formally grounded work on many aspects of CG. Klein and van Benthem (1987), the joint proceedings of workshops held in Amsterdam and Stirling in June 1987, includes papers on type theory (Calder, Hendriks, Ponse) and 'Lambek theorem proving' (the use of a Gentzen sequent calculus as a proof system for the validity of sentences in the Lambek calculus – more on this below) (Moortgat) as well as other foundational concerns, cross-theoretic comparisons and detailed data description. The biennial Amsterdam Colloquium is a regular focus for the best research of this kind (see, for example, Groenendijk *et al.* 1987), and van Benthem and Moortgat are probably at present its most important proponents.

Nor is logical research restricted to mainland Europe. Many of the original leaders of 'Montague Grammar' – Barbara Partee, Emmon Bach, David Dowty and others – are still active. A newer wave, inspired more by Lambek than Montague, is centred on Edinburgh, including work by Glyn Morrill, Guy Barry, Mark Hepple and others on the logical and type-theoretic foundations of CG and their applications in linguistic description: Morrill *et al.* (1990) look at the Gentzen sequent calculus but prefer, as more readable, the proof figures of 'natural deduction', and Leslie (1990) compares both these with 'proof nets'. And conceptually – as I hope will be clear by now – although many linguists may well not want to follow the fine grain of the logical arguments, their results form the essential foundations for any sound, principled categorial linguistic description.

Somewhat different from this rather abstract appeal to logic, there is a growing body of computational work with a logical foundation, under the banner of 'parsing as deduction'. This will be discussed with more general computational work (Ch.6.vi).

6.v COMPLEXITY

It is typical of another, closely related line in the ancestry of CGs that Lambek (1988: 311) could ask as a rhetorical question, with four dense pages of affirmative answer, 'What conceivable applications are there of biclosed monoidal categories to linguistics?' The explicitly algebraic aspects of CG were more important than semantics to such pioneers as Lambek and Bar-Hillel, and are evident as far back as Frege – who was, after all, concerned with mathematical logic – and indeed the algebra and logic of CG remain closely linked. They remain a major factor in its appeal for formally minded, and especially computational, linguists. Related quite naturally to these more formal concerns, although not peculiar to CGs, is the question of formal complexity: the early history of CG was heavily negatively influenced by proofs of the formal equivalence of various systems, and more recently there has been a positive convergence of effort in the search for a minimally context-sensitive calculus.

The algebra of CGs is found at its purest, perhaps, in the work of Lambek (1958, 1988), developed by Buszkowski (e.g. 1987, 1988a, 1988b). Lambek's theory, as we have seen (Ch.2.iii.a above), is explicitly set out as a deductive calculus, and 'employs an algebraic framework from the very beginning, as it uses residuation algebra operations to define categories' (Buszkowski 1988b: 68); Buszkowski has worked out various properties and consequences of the Lambek calculus, to some of which we will return. As a decision procedure – 'an effective method for testing whether a sentence of the syntactic calculus is deducible from [the] rules' (Lambek 1958 [1988]: 165) – Lambek adopts 'the decision procedure discovered by Gentzen for the intuitionistic propositional calculus' (ibid.). I do not propose to give an explanation here of the Gentzen sequent calculus, which Lambek himself (ibid.) explains clearly enough for the interested reader. It is worth mentioning, however, as it has been taken up by van Benthem (1988a, 1988b, etc.), Moortgat (1988b), Morrill (e.g. Morrill *et al.* 1990), and others as a format for proofs of validity of rules, formulae or sentences.

Given the clear mathematical foundation of CG, it is only natural that complexity and formal equivalence results for various calculi should have been significant in its development from an early stage. Bar-Hillel *et al.*'s (1960) proof of the weak equivalence of either a unidirectional or bidirectional application-only 'AB' (Ajdukiewicz/ Bar-Hillel) grammar to a context-free phrase-structure grammar was a serious blow to its acceptance at the time as being of any linguistic interest. Two factors should be distinguished here. First, formal equivalence was, and too often still is, thought of as grounds for dismissal of the (for whatever reason) less favoured 'variant'. Pollard (1988: 394) still feels the need to make the explicit point – with an entirely appropriate analogy – that:

> notational variants naturally suggest different kinds of mathematical variants and generalizations. An analogy with abstract algebra may help make this point. It is well known that there is a category isomorphism between the theory of boolean algebras and the theory of boolean rings. For every theorem of boolean algebra, there is a corresponding theorem about boolean rings, and conversely. But the natural extension of boolean algebra is general lattice theory, while the extension of boolean rings leads to the general algebra of rings. Neither of these more general theories is in any sense a notational variant of the other.

Second, linguists until relatively recently accepted Chomsky's arguments that natural language required a grammar of more than context-free power. If a context-free phrase-structure grammar was inadequate to describe language, then an equivalent CG would be also. Either framework, to reach even descriptive adequacy, would have to be extended. Chomsky had his extensions – transformations – ready to hand. Lambek's calculus was available as an extension of CG, but the categorial enterprise was further set back by a proof by Cohen (1967) of the weak equivalence of the full Lambek calculus to an Ajdukiewicz/Bar-Hillel grammar and thus, again, to a context-free phrase-structure grammar, which was not shown to be defective until Zielonka (1978) and Buszkowski (1985). Unfortunately neither *Studia Logica* nor *Zeitschrift für mathematische Logik und Grundlagen der Mathematik* is widely read among linguists, and in any case by then the damage had been done, and 'classical' CGs had been largely written off as incapable of linguistically interesting results.

The exact power of the Lambek calculus is in fact still, at the time of writing, not determined. But meanwhile the weight of evidence has come to show that natural language is, for the most part, context-free, and that the few exceptional constructions are so exceptional as strongly to suggest that they demand equally exceptional riders to an essentially context-free description language (see Gazdar and Pullum 1985). 'And so it could come about that recently a sympathetic linguist discussing Lambek categorial grammar could admit its attractions "but for the still unallayed fear that it might not be context-free"' (van Benthem 1988b: 27).

With the change in our understanding of the formal complexity of natural language, the question of the power of grammars has taken on a new significance for all linguistic theories. Work by Stuart Shieber has illuminated the equivalences among the principal unification-based grammar formalisms (see Shieber 1987 for a discussion focusing on LFG and GPSG), and Aravind Joshi has explored what he calls the 'convergence of mildly context-sensitive grammar formalisms' (Joshi 1987) – a promising field, as the mildly context-sensitive languages keep many of the appealing features of the context-free languages. This is exactly the consensus we have seen within the categorial spectrum – the need for a calculus which minimally exceeds context-free power – despite the disagreements, which we have also seen, over how to achieve it. The suspected, then proven context-sensitive power of generalized composition (see Ch.4.iii.a above) has led some to hedge it in with category-specific constraints, others to abandon it in favour of other devices, such as wrapping rules, which then, of course, need their own constraints.

If the final ground for choice here – to be honest – is still subjective and aesthetic, it has a firmer foundation than in many areas of many linguistic theories. A great deal of work continues to be done investigating the formal powers of various categorial calculi, themselves readily defined (from their beginning, as we have seen) by the range of unary and binary rules they include. Again, several of the papers in Buszkowski *et al.* (1988) are illuminating. For example, Kandulski (1988) explores the properties of a Lambek calculus without the laws of associativity. Chytil and Karlgren (1988) discuss a generalized CG in which any linguistic string can have an infinite number of categories, but varying restrictions on the maximum length of categories (i.e. the number of symbols they may contain) correspond to independently known measures of varying 'degree of context-sensitivity'. In Oehrle *et al.*, van Benthem (1988a) studies a 'commutative', permutation-closed variant of the Lambek calculus, and Buszkowski gives a particularly valuable survey of recent results concerning the strong and weak generative power of classical and Lambek CGs. This is not the place for the details of these results – most linguists would echo Cresswell's comment on a proof by Gaifman, 'I understood it, I think, when I read it but I quickly forgot it' (quoted by Buszkowski 1988b: 82). The important general point is that formal complexity, increasingly recognized as a significant metric for any grammar, is both naturally investigated and increasingly well understood for a wide range of CGs.

6.vi PARSING

A large proportion of current work on CG is either directly computational or heavily influenced by computational considerations. Bar-Hillel, who was probably the first serious computational linguist, turned to CGs for their inherently arithmetical nature, which made them more obvious candidates for implementation than any other available grammar formalism. Parsing with an AB, application-only CG is indeed a straightforward operation, apart from the problem – surprisingly neglected, given its importance – of choosing among the possible category assignments for a word.

A second problem begins to arise when the grammar is extended in the interests of descriptive adequacy, for these same extensions – either simple function composition or type-raising by itself would be enough – lead to the possibility of multiple derivation paths, semantically identical, for the same input string. This is the problem known as 'spurious ambiguity' – 'ambiguity' because a parser must choose among (an embarrassing wealth of) alternative possible moves, 'spurious' because they all lead to the same result – which has been widely addressed, in a number of rather different ways. The third issue (not a problem!) to be touched on here is the growing body of logically inspired work on 'parsing as deduction'.

Even phrase-structure grammars with small numbers of syntactic categories, all atomic, and therefore largely uninformative, have to face the problem that the lexicons of (at least) many natural languages include (at least) many words with more than one possible category assignment. Noun–verb alternation in English is a notorious instance of this, giving rise to such examples of global ambiguity as the classic *Time flies* and my own favourite *Guardian* headline *Hattersley courts import curbs controversy*, as well as innumerably common local parsing ambiguities.

In a CG this problem is exacerbated by two factors. First, even in a calculus with no unary type-changing rules, the richer information content and thus finer grain of CG categories means that one phrase-structure grammar category often corresponds to more than one in CG. Most conspicuously, an English 'verb' can be $S\backslash NP$, $(S\backslash NP)/NP$ or $((S\backslash NP)/NP)/NP$, and quite a few of them are more than one of these (transitive/intransitive verbs like *eat* or *read*, in particular). As far as I know, only Chytil and Karlgren (1988) give serious consideration to this problem, proposing that analysis and category assignment should be interleaved:

> Though it often seems as though categorial symbols were first
> assigned in one pass prior to cancellation ... assignment and can-
> cellation must in any actual algorithm be interwoven: it is in
> practice necessary to look ahead at cancellation when making
> the assignment. ... The category is obtained as a result of the
> computation, not as its starting point.
>
> (1988: 88)

This is reminiscent of the success of mixed-mode (top-down/
bottom-up) parsers for phrase structure grammars, with assignment
acting (effectively) top-down, expectation driven, and cancellation
data-driven, bottom-up; Marcus (1980) gives the classic pioneering
argument for such 'mixed' parsing algorithms.

Second, as soon as recursive type-change (by unbounded raising
and/or division) is a possibility, the number of options becomes
infinite: that is, if these rules are interpreted as well-formedness conditions on lexical assignments, then an infinite number of types must
be assigned to words in the lexicon; if the rules are procedural ones
available to the parser as operations, there is equally an infinite space
of possible procedurally derived assignments. This aspect of the
problem has received rather more attention, as those who propose
open-ended raising systems tend to be aware of the dangers in their
proposals. Thus Rooth and Partee (1982) and Partee and Rooth
(1983) have been widely followed (e.g. by Dowty 1988) in their
strategy of minimal type assignments. Others have reacted by not
allowing raising rules in their grammars at all: however, this is more
often with an eye to the proliferation of derivation paths that can be
induced by raising than to the initial problem of determining the
category assignment, and so falls more properly under the second
major problem, that of spurious ambiguity.

The problem of category assignment in CG could fairly be called
linguistic, in its tie to the facts of natural language, and (therefore) in
its comparability to the same problem in other theories. The problem
of spurious ambiguity, however, is entirely a parsing problem, and
peculiar to generalized CGs. It was recognized, in the abstract, long
before it became a computational issue and therefore a problem —
thus Geach, discussing the consequences of his division rule (see
Ch.3.v above):

> Such possibilities of multiple analysis do not mean that we have

a syntactically ambiguous string. We have a single 'proper series of indices' ... for a given sentence; the different ways of multiplying out the indices reveal two different but equally legitimate ways of dissecting out an S[yntactically] C[onnex] sub-string from a larger SC string.

(1972: 485)

While this remained an abstract, or declarative, characteristic of generalized CGs, it was simply an interesting fact; or even, positively, the key to the possibility of describing many cases of non-standard 'constituency'. As soon as such grammars were implemented it became a nightmare. A naive non-deterministic parser would insist on following every possible derivation path, which in the worst case would multiply exponentially in the length of the input string, rapidly resulting in totally intractable parse times. To cut this off by stopping after finding the first complete derivation would be to lose all possibility of detecting genuine semantic ambiguities. Somehow, a categorial parser needed to find one and only one derivation path for each semantic interpretation. As computational work on CGs became more prevalent, this problem became more urgent, and it is no cause for surprise – nor for pride – that a number of different proposals and counter-proposals have been put forward, restricting or augmenting the calculus or the parsing algorithm in various ways, of which a small, reasonably representative sample follows. For details and further references the reader is referred to the original sources cited.

One common strategy is to impose incremental interpretation as the parsing strategy. This is appealing on grounds of psychological plausibility, and also on computational grounds of processing efficiency, the more so as it can approximate determinism (Marcus 1980 carries this approach through to its logical conclusion in a psg framework). Spurious ambiguity will be eliminated if for every distinct interpretation the parser finds an entirely incremental, left-branching derivation path. One means to this is the use of composition, as pointed out in Ades and Steedman (1982): this makes available, in principle, a multitude of semantically equivalent derivations, but the operations of a parser can be constrained to work left-to-right bottom-up so as to find only the left-branching one.

Pareschi and Steedman (1987) point out the problem that this may not make available the 'constituents' to which postmodifiers apply: in their example *John loves Mary madly*, *madly* is of category **VP\VP**, modifying the **VP** *loves Mary*, but that **VP** has never been derived as such. Their solution relies on the procedural, or parametric, neutrality of combinatory rules to 'recover' the **VP** from within **S**, and is in fact a simpler precursor of Steedman's 'decomposition' approach to gapping (see Ch.5.iii.e above). Wittenburg (1987) proposes, rather than recovering from such problems, ensuring that they do not arise in the first place. His system 'involves deriving a new set of combinators, termed predictive combinators, that replace the basic forms of functional composition and type raising' (1987: 73) and allow ambiguous structure to arise only where it is actually needed. Bouma (1989), on the other hand, eliminates raising rather than redefining it, using instead application, composition and a number of simple inference rules for the use of products to give a calculus which, being structurally complete, can produce a strictly left-branching derivation for every reading of a sentence. A somewhat different approach, to which we will return shortly, is taken by Hepple and Morrill (1989).

In conclusion, more positively, a notable fusion of the logical roots of the categorial tradition with its most recent computational flowering can be found in the school of 'parsing as deduction'. A grammar is seen as a proof system, its rules as axioms and sentences as theorems to be proved on the basis of those axioms. Michael Moortgat has been a principal proponent, developing Lambek's suggestion of the Gentzen sequent calculus as a suitable framework for proofs of the grammaticality or otherwise of sentences under a given CG (see especially Part Two of Moortgat 1988b, 'Categorial parsing as Gentzen deduction'). Along slightly different lines, Pareschi (1988) encodes categorial types as definite clauses in a slightly modified Horn clause logic with a natural Prolog implementation. And this proof-theoretic approach also offers a possible solution to the problem of spurious ambiguity: Hepple and Morrill (1989) propose that familiar notions of reduction of proofs to normal form can be applied to derivations.

> With grammar regarded as analogous to logic, derivations are proofs; what we are advocating is proof-reduction, and normal form proof; the invocation of these logical techniques adds a further paragraph to the story of parsing-as-deduction.
>
> (1989: 10)

It remains only for these results to come out of their logical corner and be made more accessible to the non-specialist – at the moment even their notation (to say nothing of their value) is clear to only a minority even of categorial grammarians, let alone the wider community. Work is needed which links these techniques firmly into real linguistic description, well beyond the now customary hand-wave at non-constituent co-ordination. Systematically to apply these advances in the formal and computational framework to the gaps in the linguistic coverage of CGs would be a significant contribution to our formal understanding of natural language.

7 Overview and prospect

So how can one summarize the accomplishments and prospects of categorial grammars, their strengths and weaknesses and their standing among the current major linguistic theories?

CGs are a long way from offering anything like a complete description of any language, or any consensus as to how to do so. A great deal of work is now being done, with great energy, enthusiasm and intelligence, but much of it seems to be galloping off in all directions at once. To quote two of the editors of one of the most important recent sources, Buszkowski *et al.* (1988):

> As a matter of fact, categorial grammar still remains in a pre-theoretical stage of development. Surely, there have appeared numerous deep elaborations of different relevant topics; it would be hard even to mention them all. The authors, however, usually confined themselves to certain particular aspects with no attempt to draw a complete picture.
>
> (Buszkowski 1988b: 57)

> At the present moment, it is certainly too early to speak of a well-crystallized new categorial grammar. Too much remains to be explored, too much to be understood about what has been explored already.
>
> (van Benthem 1988b: 27)

Throughout this survey I have commented repeatedly on both the patchiness and the diversity of current work in CG. The patchiness shows mainly in the collective linguistic coverage so far available, which, although as a list of languages and topics it looks impressive (see the introduction to Ch. 5), on closer inspection has significant gaps, especially when it comes to the more common, mundane, even boring – but necessary – facts of natural language(s). There is little or no recent work on passives or raising, questions, imperatives, noun-phrase structure, adverbials and so on, let alone such broad areas as information structure, pragmatics or text grammars. The diversity undermines such work as has been done, which even in the better-represented areas is likely to be cast in incompatible versions of the wider framework or to be internally in dispute.

On the other hand, the foundational principles of CGs, both formal and informal, are better understood and more explicitly respected than in many other theories, which gives cause for optimism. A theory which has heaped extensive, generally accepted descriptions of natural language(s) on shaky foundations and tries later to underpin them – castles on sand, one is tempted to say – must stand less of a chance than a theory which has, as yet, built a somewhat sprawling and leaky structure on a solid base. Diversity here is healthy – productive investigation is continuing into many different aspects of CGs, reflecting the many concerns that have fed into it over the years and continue to do so: logic, algebra, philosophy of language and formal semantics, language-specific and universal syntax, psycholinguistics and computational linguistics. The best work in CG shows a creative balance of these considerations to a degree rarely matched within other paradigms.

If CGs are distinctive in this foundational richness, their cause has also been advanced by awareness of their compatibility, in many respects, with other major current linguistic theories. The convergence has come in a number of ways. GPSG and LFG, in particular, have adopted a Montague(-like) semantics and mechanisms for encoding something like function–argument relations (the Control Agreement Principle of GPSG and, although less clearly, the up- and down-arrow 'meta-variables' of LFG). A more careful understanding of the formal properties of natural languages and of grammars has led to CGs being taken more seriously and aligned more accurately relative to proposals in other frameworks.

Meanwhile, the encoding of CGs in a unification-based formalism has opened the way for their participation in the general convergence of 'unification grammars' over the last few years. Theory-neutral unification-based programming environments like PATR-II (Shieber 1984, 1986), drawing on a wide range of theories, have facilitated the convergence:

> With the development of an expressive and formally precise *lingua franca*, essentially the full range of current theories can

be composed, decomposed, compared, recombined, and generally tinkered with, in a manner constrained only by the
individual researcher's aesthetic sense, philosophical predisposi-
tions, and responsibility to get the facts right.

(Pollard and Sag 1987: 11)

And thence specific theories have emerged which are eclectic hybrids;
most notably Pollard and Sag's Head-driven Phrase Structure
Grammar, which 'freely avails itself of ideas from categorial
grammar, discourse representation theory, generalized phrase structure grammar, government–binding theory, lexical-functional
grammar, and situation semantics' (1987: v). Of HPSG's 'proposed
principles of universal grammar', the 'Head Feature Principle' and
the 'Binding Inheritance Principle' are effectively the Head Feature
Convention and the Foot Feature Principle of GPSG, while the
'Subcategorization Principle' 'is essentially a generalization of the
"argument cancellation" employed in categorial grammar' (ibid.: 11),
and grammatical relations are similarly defined on the (underlying)
order of cancellation. This is certainly as clear a sign as one could find
of the importance of the contribution that CGs can make to the
general development of linguistic theory, and of the respect they are
increasingly afforded.

But the future of categorial grammars is surely not just as an
ingredient in theory-salads – however significant an ingredient, and
however substantial a dish the salads are. Their foundations are firm
enough, and the momentum of current work strong enough, for the
many undoubted omissions and disagreements to be made good, not
overnight, but on a perfectly reasonable timescale for such enter-
prises, as long as categorial grammarians are willing to focus their
energies on agreed accounts of bread-and-butter language rather than
squabbling over cream puffs. The last word should go to Johan van
Benthem (1988a: 65):

After all, if one takes the categorial perspective seriously, then,
why should it always have to prove itself by comparison with its
generative rival? ... Perhaps, it is time to start changing the
textbooks.

References

Ades, Anthony and Mark Steedman (1979) 'On word-order', ms., University of Warwick.

—— (1982) 'On the order of words', *Linguistics and Philosophy* 4:517–58.

Ajdukiewicz, Kazimierz (1935) 'Die syntaktische Konnexität', *Studia Philosophica* 1:1–27; translated as 'Syntactic connexion', in S. McCall (ed.), *Polish Logic*, Oxford, 1967, pp. 207–31.

Bach, Emmon (1977) 'Comments on a paper by Chomsky', in Peter Culicover, Thomas Wasow and Adrian Akmajian (eds), *Formal Syntax*, New York: Academic Press, pp. 133–55.

—— (1979a) 'Montague Grammar and classical transformational grammar', in Steven Davis and Marianne Mithun (eds), *Linguistics, Philosophy, and Montague Grammar*, Austin: University of Texas Press, pp. 3–49.

—— (1979b) 'Control in Montague Grammar', *Linguistic Inquiry* 10:515–31.

—— (1980) 'In defense of passive', *Linguistics and Philosophy* 3:297–341.

—— (1982) 'Purpose clauses and control', in Pauline Jacobson and Geoffrey Pullum (eds), *The Nature of Syntactic Representation*, Dordrecht: Reidel, pp. 35–57.

—— (1984) 'Some generalizations of categorial grammars', in Fred Landman and Frank Veltman (eds), *Varieties of Formal Semantics*, Dordrecht: Foris, pp. 1–23.

—— (1987) 'Categorial grammars and natural languages', first joint meeting of the Association for Symbolic Logic and the Linguistic Society of America, Stanford, CA, July 1987.

—— (1988) 'Categorial grammars as theories of language', in Richard Oehrle, Emmon Bach and Deirdre Wheeler (eds), *Categorial Grammars and Natural Language Structures*, Dordrecht: Reidel, pp. 17–34.

Bar-Hillel, Yehoshua (1953) 'A quasi-arithmetical notation for syntactic description', *Language* 29:47–58; reprinted in Y. Bar-Hillel, *Language and Information*, Reading, MA: Addison-Wesley, 1964, pp. 61–74.

—— (1960) 'Some linguistic obstacles to machine translation', in *Advances in Computers*, vol. I. New York: Academic Press; Reprinted in Y. Bar-Hillel, *Language and Information*, Reading, MA: Addison-Wesley, 1964, pp. 75–86.

—— (1962) 'Four lectures on algebraic linguistics and machine translation', in Y. Bar-Hillel, *Language and Information*, Reading, MA: Addison-Wesley, 1964, pp. 185–218.

Bar-Hillel, Yehoshua, C. Gaifman and E. Shamir (1960) 'On categorial and phrase structure grammars', *The Bulletin of the Research Council of Israel* 9F:1–16; reprinted in Y. Bar-Hillel, *Language and Information*, Reading, MA: Addison-Wesley, 1964, pp. 99–115.

Barry, Guy and Martin Pickering (1990) 'Dependency and constituency in categorial grammar', in Guy Barry and Glyn Morrill (eds), *Studies in Categorial Grammar* (Edinburgh Working Papers in Cognitive Science 5), Centre for Cognitive Science, University of Edinburgh, pp. 23–45.

Barwise, Jon and John Perry (1983) *Situations and Attitudes*, Cambridge, MA: MIT Press.

van Benthem, Johan (1987a) 'Semantic type change and syntactic recognition', University of Amsterdam Department of Mathematics Report 87-05.

—— (1987b) 'Categorial grammar and type theory', ITLI Prepublication Series 87-07, University of Amsterdam.

—— (1988a) 'The Lambek calculus', in Richard Oehrle, Emmon Bach and Deirdre Wheeler (eds), *Categorial Grammars and Natural Language Structures*, Dordrecht: Reidel, pp. 35–68.

—— (1988b) 'New trends in categorial grammar', in Wojciech Buszkowski, Witold Marciszewski and Johan van Benthem (eds), *Categorial Grammar*, Amsterdam: John Benjamins, pp. 23–33.

Bird, Steven (ed.) (1991) *Declarative Perspectives on Phonology* (Edinburgh Working Papers in Cognitive Science 7), Centre for Cognitive Science, University of Edinburgh.

Bird, Steven and Ewan Klein (1990) 'Phonological events', *Journal of Linguistics* 26:33–56.

Bouma, Gosse (1986a) 'Grammatical functions and agreement in Warlpiri', in F. Beukema and A. Hulk (eds), *Linguistics in the Netherlands 1986*, Dordrecht: Foris, pp. 19–26.

—— (1986b) 'Warlpiri wildness: a categorial study of free word-order', Master's thesis, Rijksuniversiteit Groningen.

—— (1987) 'A unification-based analysis of unbounded dependencies in categorial grammar', in J. Groenendijk, M. Stokhof and F. Veltman (eds), *Proceedings of the Sixth Amsterdam Colloquium*, Amsterdam: ITLI, pp. 1–19.

—— (1989) 'Efficient processing of flexible categorial grammar', *Proceedings of EACL89*, Manchester: Association for Computational Linguistics, pp. 19–26.

Bresnan, Joan (1978) 'A realistic transformational grammar', in Morris Halle, Joan Bresnan and George Miller (eds), *Linguistic Theory and Psychological Reality*, Cambridge, MA: MIT Press, pp. 1–59.

—— (ed.) (1982) *The Mental Representation of Grammatical Relations*, Cambridge, MA: MIT Press.

Bresnan, Joan and Ronald M. Kaplan (1982) 'Introduction: grammars as mental representations of language', in Joan Bresnan (ed.), *The Mental Representation of Grammatical Relations*, Cambridge, MA: MIT Press, pp. xvii–lii.

Bresnan, Joan, Ronald M. Kaplan, Stanley Peters and Annie Zaenen (1982) 'Cross-serial dependencies in Dutch', *Linguistic Inquiry* 13:613–636.

Buszkowski, Wojciech (1985) 'The equivalence of unidirectional Lambek grammars and context-free grammars', *Zeitschrift für mathematische Logik und Grundlagen der Mathematik* 31:369–84.

—— (1987) 'Discovery procedures for categorial grammars', in Ewan Klein and Johan van Benthem (eds), *Categories, Polymorphism and Unification*, Centre for Cognitive Science, University of Edinburgh, and Institute for Logic, Language, and Information, University of Amsterdam, pp. 35–64.

—— (1988a) 'Generative power of categorial grammars', in Richard Oehrle, Emmon Bach and Deirdre Wheeler (eds), *Categorial Grammars and Natural Language Structures*, Dordrecht: Reidel, pp. 69–94.

—— (1988b) 'Three theories of categorial grammar', in Wojciech Buszkowski, Witold Marciszewski and Johan van Benthem (eds), *Categorial Grammar*, Amsterdam: John Benjamins, pp. 57–84.

Buszkowski, Wojciech, Witold Marciszewski and Johan van Benthem (eds) (1988) *Categorial Grammar*, Amsterdam: John Benjamins.

Calder, Jonathan, Mike Reape and Henk Zeevat (1989) 'An algorithm for generation in Unification Categorial Grammar', *Proceedings of EACL89*, Manchester: Association for Computational Linguistics, pp. 233–40.

154   *Categorial Grammars*

Casadio, Claudia (1988) 'Semantic categories and the development of categorial grammars', in Richard Oehrle, Emmon Bach and Deirdre Wheeler (eds), *Categorial Grammars and Natural Language Structures*, Dordrecht: Reidel, pp. 95–123.

Chierchia, Gennaro (1988) 'Aspects of a categorial theory of binding', in Richard Oehrle, Emmon Bach and Deirdre Wheeler (eds), *Categorial Grammars and Natural Language Structures*, Dordrecht: Reidel, pp. 125–51.

Chomsky, Noam (1957) *Syntactic Structures*, The Hague: Mouton.

—— (1963) 'Formal properties of grammars', in R. D. Luce, R. Bush and E. Galanter (eds), *Handbook of Mathematical Psychology*, vol. II, New York and London: John Wiley, pp. 323–418.

—— (1965) *Aspects of the Theory of Syntax*, Cambridge, MA: MIT Press.

Chomsky, Noam and George Miller (1963) 'Introduction to the formal analysis of natural languages', in R. D. Luce, R. Bush and E. Galanter (eds), *Handbook of Mathematical Psychology*, vol. II, New York and London: John Wiley, pp. 269–322.

Chytil, M. P. and H. Karlgren (1988) 'Categorial grammars and list automata for strata of non-CF-languages', in Wojciech Buszkowski, Witold Marciszewski and Johan van Benthem (eds), *Categorial Grammar*, Amsterdam: John Benjamins, pp. 85–112.

Cohen, Joel M. (1967) 'The equivalence of two concepts of categorial grammar', *Information and Control* 10:475–84.

Crain, Stephen and Mark Steedman (1985) 'On not being led up the garden path: the use of context by the psychological sentence processor', in David Dowty, Lauri Karttunen and Arnold Zwicky (eds), *Natural Language Parsing*, Cambridge: Cambridge University Press, pp. 320–58.

Cresswell, M. J. (1988) 'Categorial languages', in Wojciech Buszkowski, Witold Marciszewski and Johan van Benthem (eds), *Categorial Grammar*, Amsterdam: John Benjamins, pp. 113–26.

Curry, Haskell B. (1930) 'Grundlagen der kombinatorischen Logik', *American Journal of Mathematics* 52:509–36, 789–934.

—— (1950) *A Theory of Formal Deducibility* (Notre Dame Mathematical Lectures 6), University of Notre Dame.

—— (1961) 'Some logical aspects of grammatical structure', in R. O. Jakobson (ed.), *Structure of Language and its Mathematical Aspects: Proceedings of the Symposia in Applied Mathematics*, vol. XII. Providence, RI: American Mathematical Society, pp. 56–68.

Curry, Haskell B. and Robert Feys (1958) *Combinatory Logic*, vol. I, Amsterdam: North-Holland.

Davis, Steven and Marianne Mithun (eds) (1979) *Linguistics, Philosophy, and Montague Grammar*, Austin: University of Texas Press.

Dowty, David R. (1978) 'Governed transformations as lexical rules in a Montague Grammar', *Linguistic Inquiry* 9:393–426.

—— (1979a) *Word Meaning and Montague Grammar: the Semantics of Verbs and Times in Generative Semantics and Montague's PTQ*, Dordrecht: Reidel.

—— (1979b) 'Dative "Movement" and Thomason's extensions of Montague Grammar', in Steven Davis and Marianne Mithun (eds), *Linguistics, Philosophy, and Montague Grammar*, Austin: University of Texas Press, pp. 153–222.

—— (1982) 'Grammatical relations and Montague Grammar', in Pauline Jacobson and Geoffrey Pullum (eds), *The Nature of Syntactic Representation*, Dordrecht: Reidel, pp. 79–130.

—— (1985) 'On recent analyses of the semantics of control', *Linguistics and Philosophy* 8:291–331.

—— (1988) 'Type raising, functional composition, and non-constituent conjunction', in Richard Oehrle, Emmon Bach and Deirdre Wheeler (eds), *Categorial Grammars and Natural Language Structures*, Dordrecht: Reidel, pp. 153–97.

Dowty, David R., Robert E. Wall and Stanley Peters (1981) *Introduction to Montague Semantics*, Dordrecht: Reidel.

Flynn, Michael (1983) 'A categorial theory of structure building', in Gerald Gazdar, Ewan Klein and Geoffrey Pullum (eds), *Order, Concord and Constituency*, Dordrecht: Foris, 139–74.

Fodor, Janet Dean (1978) 'Parsing strategies and constraints on transformations', *Linguistic Inquiry* 9:427–73.

Ford, Marilyn, Joan Bresnan and Ronald M. Kaplan (1982) 'A competence-based theory of syntactic closure', in Joan Bresnan (ed.), *The Mental Representation of Grammatical Relations*, Cambridge, MA: MIT Press, pp. 727–96.

Foster, John C. (1990) 'A theory of word order in categorial grammar with special reference to Spanish', DPhil. dissertation, University of York.

Frege, Gottlob (1879) 'Begriffsschrift, eine der arithmetischen nachge-bildete Formelsprache des reinen Denkens'. Translated as 'Begriffs-schrift, a formula language, modelled upon that of arithmetic, for pure thought', reprinted in Jean van Heijenoort, (ed.), *From Frege to Gödel: a Source Book in Mathematical Logic, 1879–1931*, Cambridge, MA: Harvard University Press, 1967, pp. 1–82.

—— (1891) 'Funktion und Begriff', translated as 'Function and concept', in Peter Geach and Max Black (eds), *Translations from the*

Philosophical Writings of Gottlob Frege, Oxford: Blackwell, pp. 21–41.

—— (1892) 'Über Sinn und Bedeutung', translated as 'On sense and reference', in Peter Geach and Max Black (eds), *Translations from the Philosophical Writings of Gottlob Frege*, Oxford: Blackwell, pp. 56–78.

Friedman, Joyce and Ramarathnam Venkatesan (1986) 'Categorial and non-categorial languages', *Proceedings of ACL86*, Columbia, NY: Association for Computational Linguistics, pp. 75–7.

Friedman, Joyce, Dawei Dai and Weiguo Wang (1986) 'The weak generative capacity of parenthesis-free categorial grammars', *Proceedings of Coling86*, Bonn: Association for Computational Linguistics, pp. 199–201.

Gazdar, Gerald (1979) *Pragmatics: Implicature, Presupposition and Logical Form*, New York: Academic Press.

—— (1980) 'A cross-categorial semantics for coordination', *Linguistics and Philosophy* 3:407–9.

—— (1981) 'Unbounded dependencies and coordinate structure', *Linguistic Inquiry* 12:155–84.

—— (1982) 'Phrase structure grammar', in Pauline Jacobson and Geoffrey Pullum (eds), *The Nature of Syntactic Representation*, Dordrecht: Reidel, pp. 131–86.

Gazdar, Gerald and Geoffrey Pullum (1985) 'Computationally relevant properties of natural languages and their grammars', report 85-24, Stanford: CSLI.

Gazdar, Gerald, Ewan Klein, Geoffrey Pullum and Ivan Sag (1985) *Generalized Phrase Structure Grammar*, Oxford: Blackwell.

Geach, Peter (1972) 'A program for syntax', in Donald Davidson and Gilbert Harman (eds), *Semantics of Natural Language*, Dordrecht: Reidel, pp. 482–97; reprinted in Wojciech Buszkowski, Witold Marciszewski and Johan van Benthem (eds), *Categorial Grammar*, Amsterdam: John Benjamins, 1988, pp. 127–40.

Greenberg, Joseph H. (1963) 'Some universals of grammar with particular reference to the order of meaningful elements', in J. Greenberg (ed.), *Universals of Language*, Cambridge, MA: MIT Press, pp. 73–113.

Groenendijk, J., M. Stokhof and F. Veltman (eds) (1987) *Proceedings of the Sixth Amsterdam Colloquium*, Amsterdam: ITLI.

Halliday, M. A. K. (1985) *An Introduction to Functional Grammar*, London: Edward Arnold.

Hendriks, Herman (1987) 'Type change in semantics: the scope of quantification and coordination', in Ewan Klein and Johan van

Benthem (eds), *Categories, Polymorphism and Unification*, Centre for Cognitive Science, University of Edinburgh, and Institute for Logic, Language, and Information, University of Amsterdam, pp. 95–120.

Hepple, Mark (1990) 'Word order and obliqueness in categorial grammar', in Guy Barry and Glyn Morrill (eds), *Studies in Categorial Grammar* (Edinburgh Working Papers in Cognitive Science 5), Centre for Cognitive Science, University of Edinburgh, pp. 47–64.

Hepple, Mark and Glyn Morrill (1989) 'Parsing and derivational equivalence', *Proceedings of EACL89*, Manchester: Association for Computational Linguistics, pp. 10–18.

Higgins, F. R. (1976) 'The pseudo-cleft construction in English', PhD dissertation, MIT (1973), Bloomington: Indiana University Linguistics Club.

Hindley, J. and R. Seldin (1986) *Introduction to Combinators and λ-Calculus*, Cambridge: Cambridge University Press.

Hiż, H. (1968) 'Computable and uncomputable elements of syntax', in B. van Rootselaar and J. F. Staal (eds), *Logic, Methodology and Philosophy of Science*, vol. III, Amsterdam: North-Holland, pp. 239–54.

Hockett, Charles F. (1954) 'Two models of grammatical description', *Word* 10:210–31.

Hoeksema, Jack (1985) *Categorial Morphology* (Outstanding Dissertations in Linguistics), New York: Garland.

Hoeksema, Jack and Richard D. Janda (1988) 'Implications of process-morphology for categorial grammar', in Richard Oehrle, Emmon Bach and Deirdre Wheeler (eds), *Categorial Grammars and Natural Language Structures*, Dordrecht: Reidel, pp. 199–248.

Huck, Geoffrey J. (1988) 'Phrasal verbs and the categories of postponement', in Richard Oehrle, Emmon Bach and Deirdre Wheeler (eds), *Categorial Grammars and Natural Language Structures*, Dordrecht: Reidel, pp. 249–63.

Hudson, Richard A. (1982) 'Incomplete conjuncts', *Linguistic Inquiry* 13:547–50.

Husserl, Edmund (1900) *Logische Untersuchungen*, Halle: Niemeyer; translated by J. N. Findlay as *Logical Investigations*, London: Routledge & Kegan Paul, 1970.

Jackendoff, Ray (1972) *Semantic Interpretation in Generative Grammar*, Cambridge, MA: MIT Press.

Jacobson, Pauline (1990) 'Raising as function composition', *Linguistics and Philosophy* 13:423–75.

Johnson, R. L. (1987) 'Translation', in Peter Whitelock, Mary McGee Wood, Harold Somers, Rod Johnson and Paul Bennett (eds), *Linguistic Theory and Computer Applications*, London: Academic Press, pp. 257–86.

Joshi, Aravind (1987) 'The convergence of mildly context-sensitive grammar formalisms', CSLI workshop on 'Processing Linguistic Structure', Santa Cruz, CA, January.

Kandulski, M. (1988) 'The non-associative Lambek calculus', in Wojciech Buszkowski, Witold Marciszewski and Johan van Benthem (eds), *Categorial Grammar*, Amsterdam: John Benjamins, pp. 141–52.

Karlgren, H. (1978) 'Categorial grammar – a basis for a natural language calculus?', *Studia Logica* 37: 65–78.

Karttunen, Lauri (1987) 'Unification and syntatic theory', CSLI workshop on 'Processing Linguistic Structure', Santa Cruz, CA, January.

—— (1989) 'Radical lexicalism', in Mark R. Baltin and Anthony S. Kroch (eds), *Alternative Conceptions of Phrase Structure*, Chicago: University of Chicago Press, pp. 43–65.

Kay, Martin (1985) 'Parsing in Functional Unification Grammar', in David Dowty, Lauri Karttunen and Arnold Zwicky (eds), *Natural Language Parsing*, Cambridge: Cambridge University Press, pp. 251–78.

Keenan, Edward L. (1980) 'Passive is phrasal not (sentential or lexical)', in Teun Hoekstra, Harry van der Hulst and Michael Moortgat (eds), *Lexical Grammar*, Dordrecht: Foris, pp. 181–213.

Keenan, Edward L. and Alan Timberlake (1988) 'Natural language motivations for extending categorial grammar', in Richard Oehrle, Emmon Bach and Deirdre Wheeler (eds), *Categorial Grammars and Natural Language Structures*, Dordrecht: Reidel, pp. 265–95.

Klein, Ewan and Johan van Benthem (eds) (1987) *Categories, Polymorphism and Unification*, Centre for Cognitive Science, University of Edinburgh, and Institute for Logic, Language, and Information, University of Amsterdam.

Klein, Ewan and Ivan Sag (1985) 'Type-driven translation', *Linguistics and Philosophy* 8:163–202.

Kuno, Susumu (1976) 'Gapping: a functional analysis', *Linguistic Inquiry* 7:300–18.

Laduslaw, W. and D. R. Dowty (1988) 'Toward a non-grammatical account of thematic roles', in Wendy Wilkins (ed.), *Syntax and Semantics*, vol. 21: *Thematic Roles*, London: Academic Press, pp. 62–73.

Lambek, Joachim (1958) 'The mathematics of sentence structure', *American Mathematical Monthly* 65:154–70; reprinted in Wojciech Buszkowski, Witold Marciszewski and Johan van Benthem (eds), *Categorial Grammar*, Amsterdam: John Benjamins.

—— (1987) Note in Michael Moortgat, Richard T. Oehrle and Mary McGee Wood (eds), *Categorical Grammar Newsletter* 1:19.

—— (1988) 'Categorial and categorical grammars', in Richard Oehrle, Emmon Bach and Deirdre Wheeler (eds), *Categorial Grammars and Natural Language Structures*, Dordrecht: Reidel, pp. 297–318.

Leslie, Neil (1990) 'Contrasting styles of categorial derivations', in Guy Barry and Glyn Morrill (eds), *Studies in Categorial Grammar* (Edinburgh Working Papers in Cognitive Science 5), Centre for Cognitive Science, University of Edinburgh, pp. 113–26.

Lewis, David (1972) 'General semantics', in Donald Davidson and Gilbert Harman (eds), *Semantics of Natural Language*, Dordrecht: Reidel, pp. 169–218; reprinted in Barbara Partee (ed.), *Montague Grammar*, New York: Academic Press, 1976, pp. 1–50.

Lyons, John (1971) *Theoretical Linguistics*, Cambridge: Cambridge University Press.

McCawley, James D. (1979) 'Helpful hints to the ordinary working Montague grammarian', in Steven Davis and Marianne Mithun (eds), *Linguistics, Philosophy, and Montague Grammar*, Austin: University of Texas Press, pp. 103–26.

Marciszewski, Witold (1988) 'A chronicle of categorial grammar', in Wojciech Buszkowski, Witold Marciszewski and Johan van Benthem (eds), *Categorial Grammar*, Amsterdam: John Benjamins, pp. 7–21.

Marcus, Mitchell P. (1980) *A Theory of Syntactic Recognition for Natural Language*, Cambridge, MA: MIT Press.

Montague, Richard (1970) 'Universal grammar', in Richmond Thomason (ed.), *Formal Philosophy: Selected Papers of Richard Montague*, New Haven, CT: Yale University Press, 1974, pp. 222–46.

—— (1973) 'The proper treatment of quantification in ordinary English', in Richmond Thomason (ed.), *Formal Philosophy: Selected Papers of Richard Montague*, New Haven, CT: Yale University Press, 1974, pp. 247–70.

Moortgat, Michael (1987a) 'Lambek categorial grammar and the autonomy thesis', INL Working papers 87-03, Leiden.

—— (1987b) 'Lambek theorem proving', INL Working Papers 87-04, Leiden.

—— (1988a) 'Mixed composition and discontinuous dependencies', in Richard Oehrle, Emmon Bach and Deirdre Wheeler (eds), *Categorial Grammars and Natural Language Structures*, Dordrecht: Reidel, pp. 319–48.

—— (1988b) 'Categorial investigations: logical and linguistic aspects of the Lambek calculus', Dordrecht: Foris.

Morrill, Glyn (1987) 'Meta-categorial grammar', in Nicholas Haddock, Ewan Klein and Glyn Morrill (eds), *Categorial Grammar, Unification Grammar, and Parsing* (Edinburgh Working Papers in Cognitive Science 1), University of Edinburgh, pp. 1–29.

—— (1988) 'Extraction and coordination in phrase structure grammar and categorial grammar', PhD thesis, University of Edinburgh.

Morrill, Glyn, Neil Leslie, Mark Hepple and Guy Barry (1990) 'Categorial deductions and structural operations', in Guy Barry and Glyn Morrill (eds), *Studies in Categorial Grammar* (Edinburgh Working Papers in Cognitive Science 5), Centre for Cognitive Science, University of Edinburgh, pp. 1–21.

Oehrle, Richard T. (1975) 'The grammatical status of the English dative alternation', PhD dissertation, MIT.

—— (1981) 'Lexical justification', in Michael Moortgat, Harry van der Hulst and Teun Hoekstra (eds), *The Scope of Lexical Rules*, Dordrecht: Foris, pp. 210–28.

—— (1987) 'Boolean properties in the analysis of gapping', in Geoffrey Huck and Almerindo Ojeda (eds), *Syntax and Semantics*, vol. 20: *Discontinuous Constituents*, New York: Academic Press, pp. 201–40.

Oehrle, Richard, Emmon Bach and Deirdre Wheeler (eds) (1988) *Categorial Grammars and Natural Language Structures*, Dordrecht: Reidel.

Pareschi, Remo (1986) 'Combinatory grammar, logic programming and natural language processing', ms., Department of Artificial Intelligence, University of Edinburgh.

—— (1988) 'A definite clause version of categorial grammar', *Proceedings of ACL88*, Buffalo, NY: Association for Computational Linguistics, pp. 270–7.

Pareschi, Remo and Mark Steedman (1987) 'A lazy way to chart-parse with categorial grammars', *Proceedings of ACL87*, Stanford, CA: Association for Computational Linguistics, pp. 81–8.

Partee, Barbara (1973) 'Some transformational extensions of Montague Grammar', *Journal of Philosophical Logic* 2:509–34; reprinted in Barbara Partee (ed.), *Montague Grammar*, New York: Academic Press, 1975, pp. 51–76.

—— (1975) 'Montague Grammar and transformational grammar', *Linguistic Inquiry* 6:203–300.

—— (ed.) (1976) *Montague Grammar*, New York: Academic Press.

Partee, Barbara and Mats Rooth (1983) 'Generalized conjunction and type ambiguity', in Rainer Bäuerle, Christoph Schwarze and Arnim von Stechow (eds), *Meaning, Use, and Interpretation of Language*, Berlin and New York: de Gruyter, pp. 361–83.

Pereira, Fernando C. N. and David H. D. Warren (1980) 'Definite clauses for language analysis', *Artificial Intelligence* 13:231–78.

Pollard, Carl J. (1988) 'Categorial grammar and phrase structure grammar: an excursion on the syntax–semantics frontier', in Richard Oehrle, Emmon Bach and Deirdre Wheeler (eds), *Categorial Grammars and Natural Language Structures*, Dordrecht: Reidel, pp. 391–415.

Pollard, Carl J. and Ivan Sag (1987) *Information-based Syntax and Semantics*, Stanford: CSLI.

Postal, Paul M. (1974) *On Raising: One Rule of English Grammar and Its Theoretical Implications*, Cambridge, MA: MIT Press.

Potts, Timothy C. (1988) 'Fregean grammar: a formal outline', in Wojeich Buszkowski, Witold Marciszewski and Johan van Benthem (eds), *Categorial Grammar*, Amsterdam: John Benjamins, pp. 221–42.

Reichl, Karl (1982) *Categorial Grammar and Word-Formation: The Deadjectival Abstract Noun in English*, Tübingen: Max Niemeyer.

Reyle, Uwe and Christian Rohrer (eds) (1988) *Natural Language Parsing and Linguistic Theories*, Dordrecht: Reidel.

Roeper, T. and M. E. A. Siegel (1978) 'A lexical transformation for verbal compounds', *Linguistic Inquiry* 9:199–260.

Rooth, Mats and Barbara Partee (1982) 'Conjunction, type ambiguity, and wide scope "Or"', in D. Flickinger, M. Macken and N. Wiegand (eds), *Proceedings of the First West Coast Conference on Formal Linguistics*, Stanford: Stanford University Press, pp. 353–62.

Ross, John R. (1967) 'Constraints on variables in syntax', doctoral dissertation, MIT.

—— (1970) 'Gapping and the order of constituents', in Manfred Bierwisch and Karl Erich Heidolph (eds), *Progress in Linguistics*, The Hague: Mouton, pp. 249–59.

Šaumjan, S. K. (1973) 'The genotype language and formal semantics', in F. Kiefer (ed.), *Trends in Soviet Theoretical Linguistics* (FL Suppl. Series 18), Dordrecht: Reidel, pp. 251–333.

de Saussure, Ferdinand (1973) *Cours de linguistique générale*, Paris: Payot.

Schmerling, Susan F. (1982) 'The proper treatment of the relationship between syntax and phonology', *Texas Linguistic Forum* 19:151–66.

—— (1983) 'Montague morphophonemics', in J. F. Richardson, M. Marks and A. Chukerman (eds), *Papers from the Parasession on the Interplay of Phonology, Morphology and Syntax*, Chicago: Chicago Linguistic Society, pp. 222–37.

Schönfinkel, Moses (1924) 'Über die Bausteine der mathematischen Logik', *Mathematische Annalen* 92:305–16.

Selkirk, Elisabeth O. (1981) 'English compounding and the theory of word structure', in Michael Moortgat, Harry van der Hulst and Teun Hoekstra (eds), *The Scope of Lexical Rules*, Dordrecht: Foris, pp. 229–77.

Shieber, Stuart M. (1984) 'The design of a computer language for linguistic information', in *Proceedings of the Tenth International Conference on Computational Linguistics*, Stanford, CA: pp. 326–66.

—— (1986) *An Introduction to Unification-based Approaches to Grammar*, Stanford, CA: CSLI.

—— (1987) 'Separating linguistic analyses from linguistic theories', in Peter Whitelock, Mary McGee Wood, Harold Somers, Rod Johnson and Paul Bennett (eds), *Linguistic Theory and Computer Applications*, London: Academic Press, pp. 1–36; also in Uwe Reyle and Christian Rohrer (eds), *Natural Language Parsing and Linguistic Theories*, Dordrecht: Reidel, 1988, pp. 33–68.

Soboleva, P. A. (1973) 'Derivational structure of the Russian lexicon', in F. Kiefer (ed.), *Trends in Soviet Theoretical Linguistics* (FL Suppl. Series 18), Dordrecht: Reidel, pp. 77–103.

Steedman, Mark (1983) 'A categorial syntax for subject and tensed verb in English and some related languages', ms., University of Warwick.

—— (1984) 'On the generality of the nested-dependency constraint and the reason for an exception in Dutch', in Brian Butterworth, Bernard Comrie and Östen Dahl (eds), *Explanations for Language Universals*, Berlin: Mouton, pp. 35–66.

—— (1985a) 'Dependency and coordination in the grammar of Dutch and English', *Language* 61:523–68.

—— (1985b) 'LFG and psychological explanation', *Linguistics and Philosophy* 8:359–85.

—— (1987) 'Combinatory grammars and parasitic gaps', *Natural Language and Linguistic Theory* 5:403–39.

—— (1988) 'Combinators and grammars', in Richard Oehrle, Emmon Bach and Deirdre Wheeler (eds), *Categorial Grammars and Natural Language Structures*, Dordrecht: Reidel, pp. 417–42.

—— (1990) 'Gapping as constituent coordination', *Linguistics and Philosophy* 13:207–63.

—— (1991a) 'Type-raising and directionality in combinatory grammar', *Proceedings of ACL91*, Berkeley, CA: Association for Computational Linguistics, pp. 71–8.

—— (1991b) 'Structure and intonation', *Language* 67:260–98.

Steele, Susan (1988) 'A typology of functors and categories', in Richard Oehrle, Emmon Bach and Deirdre Wheeler (eds), *Categorial Grammars and Natural Language Structures*, Dordrecht: Reidel, pp. 443–66.

Stoy, J. (1977) *Denotational Semantics: the Scott–Strachey Approach to Programming Language Theory*, Cambridge, MA: MIT Press.

Szabolcsi, Anna (1983) 'ECP in categorial grammar', ms., Max Planck Institut für Psycholinguistik.

—— (1987) 'Bound variables in syntax (are there any?)', in J. Groenendijk, M. Stokhof and F. Veltman (eds), *Proceedings of the Sixth Amsterdam Colloquium*, Amsterdam: ITLI, pp. 331–50.

Thomason, Richmond (1974a) 'Some complement constructions in Montague Grammar', in Michael W. La Galy, Robert A. Fox and Anthony Bruck (eds), *Papers from the Tenth Regional Meeting of the Chicago Linguistic Society*, Chicago: Chicago Linguistic Society, pp. 712–22.

—— (ed.) (1974b) *Formal Philosophy: Selected Papers of Richard Montague*, New Haven, CT: Yale University Press.

—— (1976) 'Some extensions of Montague Grammar', in Barbara Partee (ed.), *Montague Grammar*, New York: Academic Press, pp. 77–117.

Uszkoreit, Hans (1986) 'Categorial Unification Grammars', *Proceedings of Coling86*, Bonn: Association for Computational Linguistics, pp. 187–94.

Vennemann, Theo and Ray Harlow (1977) 'Categorial grammar and consistent basic VX serialization', *Theoretical Linguistics* 4:227–54.

Wasow, Thomas (1977) 'Transformations and the lexicon', in Peter Culicover, Thomas Wasow and Adrian Akmajian (eds), *Formal Syntax*, New York: Academic Press, pp. 327–60.

Weir, David (1988) 'Characterizing mildly context-sensitive grammar formalisms', PhD dissertation, CIS-88-74, University of Pennsylvania.

Wheeler, Deirdre (1988) 'Consequences of some categorially-motivated phonological assumptions', in Richard Oehrle, Emmon Bach and Deirdre Wheeler (eds), *Categorial Grammars and Natural Language Structures*, Dordrecht: Reidel, pp. 467–88.

Whitelock, Peter (1988) 'A feature-based categorial morpho-syntax for Japanese', in Uwe Reyle and Christian Rohrer (eds) *Natural Language Parsing and Linguistic Theories*, Dordrecht: Reidel, pp. 230–61.

Williams, Edwin (1980) 'Predication', *Linguistic Inquiry* 11:203–38.

Winograd, Terry (1983) *Language as a Cognitive Process*, vol. 1: *Syntax*, Reading, MA: Addison-Wesley.

Wittenburg, Kent (1987) 'Predictive combinators', *Proceedings of ACL87*, Stanford, CA: Association for Computational Linguistics, pp. 73–80.

Wood, Mary McGee (1986) 'The description and processing of co-ordinate constructions', CCL/UMIST Report 86/4.

—— (1987) 'Paradigmatic rules for categorial grammars', in Ewan Klein and Johan van Benthem (eds), *Categories, Polymorphism and Unification*, Centre for Cognitive Science, University of Edinburgh, and Institute for Logic, Language, and Information, University of Amsterdam, pp. 371–81.

—— (1989) 'A categorial syntax for coordinate constructions', PhD thesis, University of London, 1988; University of Manchester Department of Computer Science Technical Report UMCSD-89-2-1.

Zeevat, Henk (1988) 'Combining categorial grammar and unification', in Uwe Reyle and Christian Rohrer (eds), *Natural Language Parsing and Linguistic Theories*, Dordrecht: Reidel, pp. 202–29.

Zeevat, Henk, Ewan Klein and Jo Calder (1987) 'Unification Categorial Grammar', in Nicholas Haddock, Ewan Klein and Glyn Morrill (eds), *Categorial Grammar, Unification Grammar, and Parsing* (Edinburgh Working Papers in Cognitive Science 1), University of Edinburgh, pp. 195–222; also *Lingua e Stile* 26.4 (1991): 499–527.

Zielonka, W. (1978) 'A direct proof of the equivalence of free categorial grammars and simple phrase structure grammars', *Studia Logica* 37:41–57.

—— (1981) 'Axiomatizability of Ajdukiewicz–Lambek calculus by means of cancellation schemes', *Zeitschrift für mathematische Logik und Grundlagen der Mathematik* 27:215–24.

Name index

Categories index

The more idiosyncratic categories are glossed with any or all of: conventional name, form of notation, author, as appropriate. Notation is given as n-d (non-directional), L (Lambek, result on top), or S (Steedman, result-first). Upper-case/lower-case variations are not significant, except the distinction between t (truth-value expression) and T (term).

Subject index